NO W...

By the same author

Sadhu Sundar Singh
Dawn in the East
God's Adventurer
Life Out of Death
Madame Guyon
Pilgrim in China

NO WAY BACK

The biography of Dr Rupert Clarke

PHYLLIS THOMSON

Phyllis Thompson

Ps 121.

Highland Books
Guildford, Surrey

Copyright © 1992 Phyllis Thompson
ISBN No: 0 946616 88 4

British Library Cataloguing-in-Publication Data. A
catalogue record for this book is available from the
British Library

Published by Highland, an imprint of Inter Publishing
Service (IPS) Ltd, Williams Building, Woodbridge Meadows,
Guildford, Surrey GU1 1BH

Typeset by Falcon Typographic Art Ltd,
Fife, Scotland
Printed in the UK by HarperCollins Manufacturing,
Glasgow.

Acknowledgements

When Rupert Clarke finished his earthly pilgrimage on 8 May 1991 his widow, Dorothea, asked me to be responsible for the memoirs he had written. With the encouragement of Edward England I made them the basis of this biography, and have quoted from them freely. In addition, my thanks are due to many of his former colleagues and friends who have provided enlightening comments and anecdotes. I am particularly grateful to his son, Major Humphrey Clarke, for his personal reminiscences and the loan of private papers.

Phyllis Thompson

Contents

Foreword

One of the privileges of being in leadership in mission is to meet individual missionaries on the spot in their locations, and to discover this one and that one, the lace of whose shoes you feel unworthy to tie.

Rupert Clarke was one of those people. Larger than life, abounding in energy and enthusiasm, totally disdaining red-tape and bureaucracy, and full of humour, he was of the kind who get on with the job while others are wondering what to do. His humour sometimes masked his deep personal concern for his fellow missionaries, a concern that endeared Uncle Ru to all those who came to know him well, from veteran workers to new missionaries. He once told us at a South Thailand Field Conference that those who had been in China and endured the sufferings and agonies of life in that land sometimes viewed us post-war come-latelies as "post-China trash". Then hastily he assured us, "but you are all wonderful post-China trash"!

Describing such a life calls for writing skills of a rare order, and all who have read Phyllis Thompson's other books will know that she is one person capable of doing it and doing it well. Today's world is impatient with missionary hero worship, and rightly so, but in painting realistic human pictures, we need to beware lest we minimise the grace of God manifested in a human life. I believe this book maintains the right balance.

May God's Spirit enable us to learn what we are meant to learn from this particular addition to the list in Hebrews chapter 11 of those who live their lives "by faith".

Denis J. Lane
International Conference Minister
Overseas Missionary Fellowship

1

He might never have been born

The doctor looked down with compassion on his patient. He knew her circumstances. Her father had died suddenly of heart failure six months previously. Her own heart was weak, she was in a very poor state of health, her husband was on half pay – and now she was pregnant again. Bills were mounting up, his own included, and until her husband, an officer in the Royal Engineers, received his new posting, they must keep up appearances on a drastically reduced income. Just at a time when she was in need of expensive nourishment and medical care, and ought to have extra help in the running of her household, too! The worry of it would do nothing to improve her health, that was obvious, and with a long pregnancy ahead of her ... The doctor shook his head dubiously, was silent for a few minutes, then made a quiet suggestion.

The pregnancy was in the very early stages. It would be a simple matter for him to terminate it. It could all be managed in the most natural way, and that would be the end of it. It could be done without difficulty. Let her talk the matter over with her husband, and if they decided to ask for his help he was prepared to give it.

So Captain Hilary Clarke and his wife talked it over. They had not wanted to start increasing their family at this awkward stage in their life, and if they agreed to the doctor's suggestion their chief problem would be solved. The tempting offer was not to be turned down lightly. There was much to be said for it. It was a private matter, involving no-one but themselves, and after all, the doctor knew what he was doing. He wouldn't have suggested it if he hadn't felt it was the right thing to do in the circumstances.

And yet . . .

They were uneasy. A new life had started, and 'abortion' was a word that was never even mentioned, except in a shamed undertone, back there in the early years of the twentieth century. Their discussion, whether short or lengthy, reached its conclusion with the decision to turn down the doctor's well-meaning offer.

'And so, in due course, I was born,' Rupert Clarke wrote many years later. 'The second of four brothers, in 1912, in Grandmother Elliott's large Victorian house in Godstone, Surrey.' And he added, 'I have often wondered what would have happened to "me" if the foetus had been washed down the drain.'

Probably his parents wondered the same thing as they saw their second son develop, knowing how easily that life might have been cut off in the womb. Not that they saw a great deal of him, as Captain Clarke's military duties often took him abroad. Although Rupert's earliest memories were of seeing a German zeppelin cruising over the sky at Ealing in the First World War, and hearing in Gillingham about the impressive military funeral of two officers who had fallen out of an aeroplane which turned upside down in a cloud, the centre of gravity for him was the Victorian house in Godstone, where Granny Elliott lived.

He came of soldier stock. His father and his grandfather were both officers in the Royal Engineers, while his great grandfather was one of the few survivors of 'the charge of the Light Brigade', having been commissioned on the field. It was taken for granted in Rupert's family that the claims of King and country must come before personal considerations. His holidays, and those of his brothers, were usually spent, not in their parents' home, wherever that happened to be, but at Godstone with Granny.

Nor were they the only ones with her there in her Victorian home. Others of her offspring were in some form of Government service, and in those days of the British Raj and the far-flung British Empire, they might be serving overseas while their children were in boarding schools in England. Sea voyages were expensive, and took too long for family reunions during the holidays, and it was almost a matter of course, in such circumstances, for the children to stay with Granny when school broke up. On one occasion a record of twenty-two cousins were being accommodated in the house in Godstone.

One of Rupert's cousins, writing years later

of the impression Rupert made in those early days, said that for her he personified the public schoolboy.

'Strong, just, never showing his feelings, always right, rather scoffing, contemptuous of weakness and condemning anything unconventional . . . I remember Rupert having to put on an Eton collar to wear at church and also, presumably at parties. It always looked so terribly uncomfortable, as if his head was imprisoned. For some reason or other, he also put it on in the nursery.

'He was always very interested in politics, and had absolutely definite ideas. I wondered where he got them from, and why everyone else's were surely wrong!'

Here at Godstone were maintained the Victorian traditions of half an hour's private prayer before breakfast, then family prayers with the servants in the dining room, and grace before meals. Bible stories and children's prayers were held after tea in the drawing room, and finally prayer kneeling alone beside one's bed before getting into it. And, of course, church on Sunday. One of the duties (considered a privilege) of the Clarke brothers was to wheel Granny there in her bath chair.

Rupert went to school at Kings College, Canterbury, which claims to have been founded by St Augustine himself, in 599 AD. 'While I remember the old buildings in the shadow of the cathedral with affection, my personal recollections of those days are not particularly happy ones. I always seemed to be in trouble. I suppose I must have been a fairly loathesome little boy, which accounted for the soreness of my caned bottom and the aching of my imposition-writing wrist. But my religious intentions had always been good, and in fact I was baptised at the age of twelve in the tiny Baptist chapel at Godstone – and later confirmed by Archbishop Lang himself in Canterbury Cathedral. On occasions of holidays in Godstone we usually cycled to the Crusader Union class in Oxted, and sometimes toyed with the idea of actually wearing a Crusader badge, but I did not actually do so at the time.' That would have been going a bit too far!

'Meanwhile, my mathematics being abysmal, I could scarcely follow the family's military profession, so it was decided that I should go in for medicine. I don't remember having been consulted about this, but I've always been very grateful for it. The switch to physics, chemistry and biology suited me well, and school became much less unenjoyable. By 1929 the Premedical Exam (1st M B) was passed and a scholarship into the Middlesex Hospital Medical School obtained.

'Here I was so appalled by the life of my fellow students – their drunkenness, immorality and bad language – that I decided to join the Christian Union as a sort of insurance policy, where I was welcomed by my seniors, Robert Pearce and Cecil Pedley.'

They took him at face value.

To all appearances he was one of them. Upright and self-controlled, morally as well as physically, he was ready unreservedly to align himself with their very small company – the Christian Union never numbered more than six members. He always conducted himself with admirable tolerance and composure in the face of open or covert sneers of contemptuous fellow students. And he seemed theologically sound. At least, he said all the right things when it came to discussions on spiritual and biblical matters. He obviously came from a thoroughly evangelical background, Rob Pearce and Cecil Pedley agreed. He could even relate how his father, when a young officer stationed at Chatham, was persuaded to attend a meeting at the Soldiers Home, where he discovered that Christianity was not just a matter of 'upholding the Raj' by attending the state church.

'Very shortly he surrendered his life to Christ, and continued to walk with Him. A few years later he attended the Keswick Convention, where he met a great-niece of Charlotte Elliott, the hymn writer. (She's the one who wrote the hymn, "Just as I am, without one plea") In due course they were married, and I was born . . .'

There was nothing one could tell Clarke about the only way of salvation being through faith in Jesus Christ that he didn't know and cordially agree with. But as they got to know him better the two came to the conclusion that there was one vitally important ingredient missing in his faith.

'He knows it all, but it still hasn't become personal. He lacks assurance', they told each other, but felt somehow that they could not tackle him about it. Clarke with his stiff military bearing, his finely chiselled nostrils and rather aloof expression was not the easiest person to approach about intimate matters. They decided to pray about it and bide their time. Eventually Cecil Pedley, instead of speaking to him about his spiritual condition, one day gave him a little booklet entitled *Safety, Certainty and Enjoyment*. It was rather dull-looking, and in some ways quite old-fashioned, but Rupert, always a perfect gentleman, accepted it courteously and placed it in his wallet. He did not read it immediately but one summer day, having time to spare, he extracted it and started to read.

'Though I had acquired considerable Bible knowledge, I still did not have any real assurance of salvation. Sometimes I felt I was right with God, and sometimes otherwise. *Safety, Certainty and Enjoyment* pointed out that my salvation in no way depended upon my feelings, but entirely upon the reliability of God's promises.' He sat there in his bedroom, slowly reading the little booklet, and the realization dawned that this was why people like Rob Pearce and Cecil Pedley were so sure. They were confident that they had eternal life, because God had asserted that everyone who believed in His Son would receive it. They had their ups and downs, their trials and disappointments like everyone else, but they never doubted that God was with them because He had promised never to forsake them.

Rupert decided that he, too, would believe, and be definite about it. There was one verse in particular on which he felt he could act. It was in the book of Revelation.

'And so I knelt by my bed and took the twentieth verse of the third chapter, "Behold, I stand at the door and knock; if any man hear my voice and open the door, I will come in to him and will sup with him, and he with Me." I just asked the Lord Jesus to come into my heart, and to stay with me.

'At that time I felt no difference at all, but thereafter I never had any doubt at all that Christ was in me, and I in Him, as it depended not on my feelings, but on the reliability of His promise.'

And he acted on his faith. No-one was left in any doubt as to what Rupert Clarke believed, and why. He always carried a Bible in his hip pocket, and was liable to quote from it freely 'and lay down the law as to what it meant. He felt he had to convert everyone he talked to,' as one of his contemporaries observed, adding rather whimsically, 'I'm afraid that he consigned some lovely people to hell without an apparent qualm!' Youthful zeal was later tempered with grace, but in those early days truth and plain speaking were delivered 'straight from the shoulder'.

He was living in Richmond, Surrey, for a period, and attending Duke Street Baptist Church, and he always said he was greatly helped by the ministry there. It was typical of the methodical Rupert that fifty years later he reported quite simply, 'I continue to pray for that church every Sunday.'

Meanwhile, medical studies were continuing, not without their setbacks. He contracted mumps while on a continental holiday with his family in 1930, 'which developed in all possible sites in my body, the swollen glands in my neck making breathing difficult, and as at the same time I had some sort of dysentery, life became singularly miserable. However, I slowly recovered under the care of Granny at Godstone ... Back at medical school in the middle of the winter term, I found that my brain was exceedingly woolly, so I suppose that I must have had encephalitis as well – the 2nd M.B. exam was a dismal failure, which put me back six months.

'In the summer of 1934 came the final MBNS exam, and when it came to the gynaecology paper I really spread myself, only to find when it came to the oral exam that the examiner had refused to read my untidy scrawl. However, six months after my failure at the final exam that hurdle was successfully cleared by paying great attention to brief answers in a legible hand, which had the desired effect on the examiners.'

His first job was as a locum in a general practice at Meopham in Kent, but it was his next move to the Sutton and Cheam Hospital which provided him with basic experience that was to stand him in good stead in years ahead.

'At that time the honorary consultant staff were all general practitioners with higher qualifications, and we dealt with a very varied spread of diseases such as would, I suppose, be impossible to cover in these more specialised days.'

The senior house officer was a Christian with whom Rupert worked in a very happy partnership. It was a time of great advance in surgery, which Rupert already found he preferred to medicine.

'The first of the antibiotic Sulfa drugs became available, and we read about, then introduced locally, the continuous intravenous saline drip, which has been so tremendously helpful to surgeons and anaesthetists ever since.

'We obtained a copy of Lorenz Bohlers text book on the treatment of fractures and were able to run a clinic on his lines. At that time also we became interested in and reasonably skilful in administering spinal anaesthetics for operations upon the lower half of the body. And we learned from him how to treat most fractures under local anaesthesia, to the great benefit of the patients – *and* of the hospital's finances.'

It was during this very busy period, when night calls for emergencies drastically reduced the time he usually spent in studying the Bible, and in prayer, that a verse in the first chapter of Paul's epistle to the Galatians gripped his attention: 'God chose me even before I was born, to reveal his son in me, that I might proclaim among the Gentiles the unsearchable riches of Christ.' He turned to a commentary and saw that the phrase 'to reveal his son in me' could also be translated 'to reveal Christ *through me*'. Suddenly the words took on a personal application. Not only through the apostle Paul was Christ to be revealed, but through him, Rupert Clarke, junior houseman in the Sutton and Cheam Hospital. Two or three weeks later, in a quiet conversation with his mother, he learned for the first time how easily he might have been aborted ... So what sort of a man ought he to be in character and conduct, to fulfil the purpose for which he had been born? He was challenged as he searched his own heart to discover his real motives, and his behaviour in the light of the Sermon on the Mount, especially when, on returning from holiday, he found that staff in the men's ward had been changed, and that the new ward sister was a rude young woman who was very difficult to work with. She went out of her way to be unco-operative, and there were occasions when Rupert was hard put to control his temper.

'But in the mercy of God I did not actually blow my top,' and he had evidently made a better impression than he realized, for one afternoon, sitting out a tennis set, he found her beside him, and in a communicative mood.

'She began to open up a bit, and revealed that she had once been engaged to a would-be missionary, but when she was unwilling to join him in this, he broke off the engagement, and eventually married someone else. I am not sure whether she was hoping for sympathy . . .' If she was, she was in for a disappointment, for she certainly got none from Rupert. On the contrary, he applauded the missionary. He had done the right thing. If he had married her it would obviously have been what was referred to in Paul's second epistle to the Corinthians, chapter six, as an 'unequal yoke,' asserted Rupert. Christians are specifically warned not to marry unbelievers, he pointed out.

The ward sister's immediate reaction was predictably 'somewhat disgruntled,' as Rupert expressed it, but his frankness bore fruit. 'It caused her to rethink her position, and a few

days later she admitted that she was from a
Christian home, but had rebelled against God.
She was now so miserable that she only longed
for courage to commit suicide.' This unexpected
confidence led to a further talk, and she was
evidently ready for it. 'When she was shown the
way back to God her rebellion collapsed, and
she was soon rejoicing in Jesus.' Eventually she
herself became a missionary – and incidentally
she kept in touch and prayed for him for the rest
of her life.

When his time at Sutton was over he decided
he needed experience in obstetrics, so took a post
in Shrewsbury as house physician in obstetrics.
'In those days the hospital had no pathologist,
and so any laboratory work had either to be
referred to London or else done ourselves – and
so some useful skills were developed by night, to
add to the routine work of the day.'

He was well set by this time on a successful
career in the field of medicine, and there seemed
nothing to hinder him from going ahead to the
fulfilment of his natural ambition to gain his
FRCS. But over the years another thought had
been turning his mind in a direction far removed
from that which would lead him to the top of his
profession in his own land. He was coming to a
spiritual crisis in his life, for, 'By this time I had
convinced myself that I should go to China with
the China Inland Mission.'

2

Call to China

In the 1930's the China Inland Mission was probably the largest and best known of the interdenominational missionary societies. The story of its founding was one to capture the imagination, for it was started one Sunday morning in 1865 by a young man on the beach at Brighton. James Hudson Taylor was not yet thirty years of age, but he had already spent several years in inland China, living and dressing as a Chinese (even to the extent of growing a pigtail), in order to proclaim the Gospel where Christ was not known. Back in England with broken health, the burden of the millions in that country who had no means of hearing that the Son of God had been made man, and died to give them everlasting life, weighed on his spirit to such an extent that he was heading for a breakdown. He felt he ought to form a missionary society to send evangelists right into the interior of the land in which dwelt nearly a quarter of the entire population of the world – but he had no financial resources, no Christian organisation or church behind him, he was merely the son of a chemist in Yorkshire, a nobody. So how could he start a missionary society? Where would the money come for the support of its workers? What would happen if they got to China, and then their health broke down, or they got into trouble with the authorities, their lives in danger . . . ?

On that historic Sunday morning, instead of going to church, he was pacing the beach at Brighton, wrestling with this problem, when the thought came to him that if God – the Almighty God – was impelling him to form a missionary society to work in inland China, then the whole responsibility of finance, health, protection, and every other need the workers might have, would be God's, not his. It was as though an intolerable weight were lifted from his mind, he felt like singing with relief and joy. Then and there, on the beach, Hudson Taylor made a definite request, praying that God would send twenty-four willing, skilful workers, to go to China. And the following day he opened a bank account in the name of China Inland Mission, with the sum of £10 – his sole capital. So China Inland Mission was started, and a year later he was on his way there with the full complement of the number he had prayed for, on a sailing ship called the *Lammermuir*.

Now, in 1934, nearly sixty years later, there were over a thousand members of the Mission working in China, and Rupert felt that he ought to add to that number by one.

At the time he entered medical school China was not in his thoughts. It was not until he was laid low with mumps that his thoughts were turned in that direction, when he was being looked after by his grandmother in Godstone.

'As I was not able to read very much, she used to come and read to me in the afternoons. Amongst the books she chose was one called, *A Thousand Miles of Miracle in China.*

'This tells the story of the Reverend Glover and his family, who were caught up in the Boxer Rebellion of 1900. They were sentenced to death in the northern province of Shansi, but the magistrate, not liking to do the job himself, passed the family on to the neighbouring magistracy, which also passed them on. Thus they were sent south, always under sentence of death, until they reached Hankow in central China, where the enlightened Chinese Viceroy put them on to a steamer to Shanghai and safety. Not all the party survived the journey, but it is a remarkable story of God's preserving power and mercy. Perhaps not ideal reading for my convalescence, but it first interested me in China.'

Then he learned that both Cecil Pedley and Rob Pearce were preparing to go there, and his interest was deepened as he read the history of the China Inland Mission written by the founder's own daughter-in-law, Mrs Howard Taylor. Rupert was in lodging with a kindly old lady at the time, doing a locum in Meopham, and did his reading with the book propped up in front of him as he ate his meals. To his surprise, his landlady, seeing what he was reading, asked if she might borrow the book when he had finished with it. The reason for her interest

was that she remembered being dandled on the
knee of Hudson Taylor himself, when she was a
little girl. 'An extraordinary coincidence,' Rupert
thought, and it helped to deepen his conviction
that he ought to go to China himself when he
was introduced by the senior physician in the
hospital where he was working to an elderly
patient who turned out to be a brother-in-law of
Hudson Taylor's sister Amelia. 'Another unexpected link with the family,' Rupert noticed. But
he realised this was not enough to constitute a
call from God.

'I was not really sure whether the China idea
was just a romantic idea of mine, or whether it
was really the will of God for my life service. And
so, when I went to do a fortnight's temporary job
in Swansea, I decided to spend my quiet times in
the morning especially to find out the answer to
this problem. To aid me in this I acquired a copy
of A T Pierson's *Life of George Muller*. It struck
me as rather a dull account of the life of a very
great man, but the chapter upon Muller's ideas
on God's guidance appeared very apposite. First
he considered "The guidance of circumstances"
which, in my case, was that I was healthy, was
not needed at home, was medically qualified, and
there seemed to be great need in China.

'Then he looked at "the general tenor of Scripture", i.e. not just one verse taken out of context
... It seemed that the command of Jesus to 'go
to all nations' applied. Then, Muller sought to
clear his mind of preconceived ideas and to pray
about the project. If he became happier in his
mind about it, he took it to be the will of God.

If he became unhappy, then he would take it that it was not the will of God for that time. I had two weeks to pray about the matter, but it only required two days for me to be quite sure that God wanted me to go to China.

'And so I began to fill in the application forms for the CIM.'

The reply he received surprised him by its promptitude. He had expected preliminaries that would spread over months before he could move forward, but instead he was invited to enter the Men's Training Home forthwith. So to Stoke Newington in north London he went, where the British headquarters of the Mission was situated, to join about half a dozen other young men all set, like himself, to go to China.

There were a few young women in training, too – but neither Rupert or any of the other men ever had a conversation with them. Indeed, they rarely even saw them. The Women's Training Home was situated several streets away, and although they all attended lectures together in the morning, the men went in first and were directed to the front, where they sat looking straight ahead, undistracted by the girls who came in demurely through another door to occupy the back seats.

It was all part of the training. They were being prepared for a land where the sexes kept apart, where men walked before women, were served first at meals, and generally took the pre-eminence. When they got to China they must wear Chinese clothes, learn the Chinese language, and perhaps most important of all, observe Chinese customs. And Chinese customs could be very rigid. The young men and women in the Training Home were left in no doubt that any friendships formed between members of the opposite sex while in training would be frowned on, and that in any case they must be prepared to remain unmarried until they had been in China for two years, and had passed the first language exam.

Those who wanted to join the Mission accepted the restriction, and as far as Rupert was concerned he did so without question – until he fell in love. Then it was not so easy.

Had it not been for the Japanese invasion of China in 1937 he would have been spared the whole disturbing affair, for he was due to sail for China that very year, and had not even met the object of his affection at this time. The Japanese invasion resulted in the postponement of the sailing of the party of new workers for a year, and Rupert decided to take a post at the Tite Street Children's Hospital in Chelsea, and at the same time attempt the examination to become a Fellow of the Royal College of Surgeons.

'This was a sad catastrophe, as three of the five questions in the main paper were on embryology, about which I had always been extremely hazy. However, the preparation for the exam was very useful, and the frequent operations for acute mastoid (a common condition still in those early days of antibiotics) proved very useful overseas.'

To what extent his mind was drawn away from the necessary study by feminine attractions it is unnecessary to surmise, but it was at this point in his career that he became, as he himself expressed it 'enamoured of one of the nurses.' He obviously took the matter very seriously, and as his advances met with a ready response it was not long before the two of them were discussing marriage. But Rupert knew that his chances of being accepted by the C I M would be very slender indeed if he married, or even became engaged, at this time. So it was decided that they would say nothing about it, but that when she had completed her nursing training she would apply to the mission 'under her own steam' and that Rupert would wait for her in China. He realized that in those circumstances marriage must be delayed for at least three or four years, but he was prepared to wait. There was nothing to prevent them from corresponding regularly, and he easily got into the habit of writing to her every week. He was always a good correspondent.

By the autumn of 1938 conditions in China were more settled, and on the first of October about a dozen young men, four of them doctors, boarded the *Express of Britain* en route for Shanghai, awaking the next morning to a gale which continued, on and off, until they reached the quiet waters of the St Lawrence River in Canada.

'Disembarking at Quebec we proceeded in rather leisurely trains to Toronto – at one stop a shunting train had to give us a push start to get going. We stayed a couple of days in Toronto, visiting the Niagera Falls on one of them, then boarded the train for the west. The first three days

were very dull, as the harvest had been reaped
and all there was to see was flat acres of wheat
stubble. But the final day was an enthralling
crossing of the Rocky Mountains, hauled by two
and pushed by one immense steam locomotives
which roared their way to the summit.

'In beautiful Vancouver we were joined by the
men recruits from North America and boarded
the *Empress of Asia* for a calm crossing of the
Pacific, arriving in Shanghai just one month after
leaving Southampton.

'It is interesting to recall that the month's
journey cost just £48, and that included full board
on the liners!'

3

In the Kansu Panhandle

Shanghai, in the year 1938, was still a very cosmopolitan city, in spite of the Japanese invasion of China. Its status as one of the Treaty Ports, with its foreign concessions and British and American gunboats moored in the Yangtse preserved it from harassment by the Japanese. The tree-lined avenues of the French concession, the expensive shops on the Nanking Road, the restaurants that specialised in old-style English cream teas all remained, as well as the famous racecourse and the fashionable clubs that catered for the tastes of professional and business men and their wives, or the officers of the armed forces stationed in the city. Motorized vehicles mingled with the man-drawn rickshaws, and the main roads were predominately westernised. The missionaries who returned from the interior in their Chinese clothes felt thoroughly out of place wearing them in Shanghai. They speedily shed them to don western style suits and dresses before going off the large compound that was the headquarters of the China Inland Mission on Sinza

Road. Its two huge buildings provided office and housing for the staff, and for the missionaries and new recruits who needed accommodation before proceeding into the interior ; to it the party of young men who disembarked from the *Empress of Asia* were promptly whisked from the quayside with its junks and boats and swarms of coolies. Rupert's impressions of Shanghai were limited.

'We were kindly entertained by the staff for a few days before boarding a coastal steamer northwards to Chefoo in Shantung province, for language study. The twenty-two of us were billeted in the sanatorium attached to the large school for missionaries' children and there we started the long process of learning the Chinese language. We had heard dismal tales of the despair of some of our predecessors, but the crisp northern air, with soccer, cricket and athletics with the schoolboys and staff kept us healthy and cheerful for the six months of language study.'

As the six months drew to a close there was an atmosphere of combined apprehension and hopeful expectation in the sanatorium. 'The Sons of the Prophets' as the young men were laughingly dubbed, were awaiting the arrival of Mr Gibb, the General Director. He was coming for the purpose of deciding where each one of them should serve. 'Designations' had been the subject of much discussion and prayer among them, for although some had strong convictions as to where they ought to go, they had all agreed to make an open offer, and abide by the General Director's decision. It might be to an old established mission centre where there was already a growing church, where Bible teaching and training in evangelism was needed. It might be to an area where pioneer work must be done. It might be in the tribal areas of the south-west, where JO Fraser had been as a apostle to the Lisu, or it might be up in the vast barren areas of Central Asia, where three intrepid women, Mildred Cable and the sisters French had travelled and lived for years, highlighting by their books the challenge of the Gobi desert dwellers.

For some the options were not likely to be so wide. Those with theological degrees knew they would probably be invited to join the staff of one or other of the Bible Schools. And the doctors knew just where the half-dozen Mission hospitals were situated – and wondered to which of them they would go.

Things worked out well for Rupert. 'I was very glad to be appointed to join my old friends Doctors Bob Pearce and Cecil Pedley at the Borden Memorial Hospital in Lanchow, capital of Kansu. Often called the Panhandle because of its shape, this province is wedged between Mongolia and Tibet, in the far north-west. Shortly after my designation we set out on a Japanese steamer for an overnight journey to Tsingtao.

'The steamer had once run on the route between Liverpool and the Isle of Man, but that was many years ago. The sea was choppy.' And forty years later he had a vivid recollection of the breakfast that was served in the early morning. He admitted that he found 'cold rice and octupus singularly uninviting.'

It was an uneventful journey by train to Kaifeng,

in the agricultural province of Henan, where many of the larger towns were already occupied by the Japanese. Their advance had been hindered, but not stopped, by the Chinese Nationalists, who had opened the banks of the Yellow River. Hundreds of miles of land had been flooded, beleaguering some of the sparsely manned Japanese garrisons; rather sporadic guerilla warfare added to the dangers of travel.

'After a night crossing of the diverted Yellow River to avoid the attention of the Japanese air force, we arrived in Chinese-held territory – although in actual fact we did not see any soldiers at all within twenty miles of the river.

'The next stage was on carts such as the Romans must have used, having a box-like body with a wheel attached at each corner, and which had to be levered round corners with a massive crow-bar.

'This was doubtless why the Romans built such straight roads,' observed Rupert drily. After about eighteen hours travel they reached Chengchow, where the railway was open to Sian.

The history of this city he found intensely interesting.

'Two hundred years before Christ it was the capital of China, after the first Emperor Ch'in had subdued all the other warring tribes; and it was he who built the amazing Great Wall from the eastern coast to the western Tibetan foothills, with the aim of keeping out the barbarians to the north. Sian was also the start of the Great Silk Road from China to Rome and the West. It was along this road that the Persian monk Alohan

came in 635 AD, to bring Christianity to China.
In the Sian museum may be seen the famous
Nestorian Stone which describes the first known
encounter of Christianity and China. At first his
message was accepted, even by the Emperor, but
in 845 AD all "foreign" religions were prohibited,
and Nestorianism was extinguished – probably
because the Bible had not been translated into
Chinese, and probably the Gospel story had been
badly mangled in two hundred years of oral
transmission.

'Sian remained the capital of China for many
years, but when we were there nothing was
known of the amazing terracotta army since
recently excavated from a royal tomb, of course.'
And in any case, the CIM party was more interested in the work of the Baptist Missionary
Society, and particularly of the hospital they had
established, which Rupert pronounced 'excellent.' He had plenty of material for the weekly
letter he wrote to the nurse in Tite Street as
he and his party continued the journey to the
north-west. They set off from Sian in an ancient
diesel bus that had to be towed along by a farm
tractor to get it started. Several days passed
before he eventually reached Lanchow, and he
made no secret of the fact that he was glad to
get there and have a good wash. Even a night
spent in the China Travel Service's 'hotel' on
Flower Family Pass was remembered mainly
because it proved to be very chilly. The last
lap of the journey had to be made without an
experienced escort, 'so our Chinese language
had its first real airing. It sufficed to get us

a good meal, but I am sure we were grossly overcharged for it.'

The walled city of Lanchow on the south bank of the Yellow River had a population of about 120,000 in 1938. Situated in the barren north-west, where the hills, devoid of vegetation for most of the year, looked like a gigantic relief map, it had frequent dust storms, blown from the Gobi desert. The houses were mostly built of sun-dried mud bricks, with roofs of a thick layer of mud and straw, supported on wooden beams. The China Inland Mission had a church and large compound inside the city, but the hospital with its men's and women's wards, staff bungalows, and separate compound for leprosy patients was on the opposite bank.

'The north bank was connected to the city by a steel bridge – the last before the river mouth 2,000 miles away. It was a tribute to the American Cleveland Bridge Company that the bridge which was built for mule carts in 1906 was standing up well to lorries and Japanese bombings so many years later.

'The hospital buildings of blue burnt bricks rose in tiers up the steep hillside, up which toiled donkeys loaded with huge buckets of murky river water, which had to be allowed to settle for a day before it could be used. After the necessary settling period to rid it of all silt, the water for use in the operating theatre was boiled in huge kettles. The Chinese have always boiled their drinking water (in readiness for the inevitable offer of tea to any guest who might enter the home) and so we had comparatively few cases

of infantile intestinal disorders, as opposed to
the usual pattern in the east.' Always observant
of cause and effect, he added in his matter-
of-fact way, 'Maybe this is why there are so
many Chinese!'

Rupert fitted in easily to the routine of hospital life, for letters from Pearce and Pedley had
prepared him, and he knew what to expect.

'Surgical instruments and medical supplies
were all very scarce, owing to the Japanese
hold upon east China, and much improvisation
was necessary to keep the work going. Supplies
of chloroform and ether being very scarce we
learned to do most of the surgery under local,
regional and spinal analgesia — which, incidentally, was much cheaper.'

'Many of the sun-denied Muslim women suf-
fered from a grave shortage of Vitamin C and
developed a softening of the bones called Osteo-
malacia, with resulting deformity of the pelvis
and difficulty in childbirth. We found by bitter
experience that these unfortunate women did
very badly when Caesarian section was performed under general, or spinal anaesthesia,
and so we turned over almost entirely to performing the operation under local anaesthesia
and this proved surprisingly satisfactory — also
for missionaries.

'Operations on the eyes and eyelids were very
common — many of them necessary because of the
vast amount of trachoma, with scratching of the
eye by in-turned eyelashes.

'Typhoid fever, louse-borne typhus fever, Mala-
Azar and tuberculosis were rife. On the other

hand, western diseases such as diabetes, high blood pressure, peptic ulcers and coronary heart disease were almost unknown.' So was appendicitis until 1941, when a modern steel-roller flour mill was moved to Lanchow to avoid the Japanese. 'Then the disorder came in almost as an epidemic – but only amongst those whose bread and noodles were made from the 'new-fangled' bran-scarce flour. We had no cases amongst our own hospital staff, who were fed upon stone-ground flour, whilst I was assured that appendicitis was common in the Government hospital, which had been recently set up, and which fed its staff with the steel-milled flour.'

In those days there were no qualified Chinese doctors or nurses on the hospital staff, only ward orderlies who received useful training in the course of their duties of caring for the patients. From time to time one or another of the doctors would go with a Chinese evangelistic team to a distant town or village, combining medical work with the preaching of the Gospel. On one of these occasions heavy rain made the road back to Lanchow impassable, and Rupert realized he could not get back to the hospital at the appointed time, and therefore would be unable to take his usual place in the schedule. He must get a message through, and let them know. Finding a telephone was not easy, but eventually he got permission to use one at the local office, and put through a call to the hospital.

He scarcely had time to announce his name,

let alone explain his reason for phoning, before
the voice at the other end of the phone burst in
with the latest news.

'Have you heard? War declared between Britain
and Germany! A British liner has been sunk by
German submarine. Bombings! An air raid on
Britain . . .'

So that is how he heard about the outbreak
of the Second World War. When he eventually
got back to Lanchow the news was filled out.
A few members of the missionary body, mainly
Americans, had receiving sets and were able
to listen in to the news. Like everyone else in
that faraway place, he had only a hazy idea of
the course of the war. He may have wondered
if it was having any effect on the nurse in
Tite Street. He could not escape the feeling
that her ardour was cooling. He wrote regularly, but her replies were getting shorter and
more irregular, and what was even more disturbing, there was a lack of spiritual content
in them. He became increasingly uneasy about
their 'understanding.' He found himself in much
the same position as the would-be missionary
who had broken off his engagement with the
ward sister. It had been easy enough for him,
when not personally involved, to assert that the
man had done the right thing, that a believer
should not marry an unbeliever. It was a more
difficult matter now. With his upbringing and
background, it went against the grain to terminate the engagement himself. A gentleman
should not jilt a lady! Eventually he decided to
make a suggestion in his next letter. Perhaps

it was not the Lord's will that they should
marry . . . ? He wondered what her reply would
be.

Meanwhile, as nothing much seemed to be
happening in Europe, life continued as usual
in China's north-west until suddenly the German armies made their spectacular advances.
Members of the hospital staff gathered appre-
hensively, day after day, around the radio to
listen to the news.

'Denmark and Norway invaded. . . .

'Holland, Belgium, Luxembourg invaded . . .

'National Government formed under Winston
Churchill . . .

'Allied troops being forced back . . . British
Expeditionary Force retreating to the beaches
. . .' It was staggering.

They heard, too, about what some called the
miracle of Dunkirk, and the successful evacu-
ation of some 340,000 officers and men across
a Channel that became strangely calm. But the
British members of the China Inland Mission in
Lanchow were left in no doubt as to the gravity of
the situation for their own country, and decided
to get in touch with the British Embassy to ask
what they should do.

'They advised us to stay on the job, as they
reckoned that our presence and assistance would
encourage the Chinese to maintain their resistance against the Japanese – and though that
was not our primary concern, we were happy
to be able to carry on. We actually saw little of
the Japanese in the far west, but occasionally
they would send over their bombers when the

moon was full. We had about four hours' warning of their raids. The only reasonable military target was the steel bridge across the river, across which came supplies of motor-fuel and ammunition from Russia, and oil from the slowly developing wells at Jade Gade, about five hundred miles west of us on the old Silk Road, along which Marco Polo came to meet Ghenghis Khan in the 13th century. It was a difficult target, well guarded by guns on the hills, and it was never damaged much.' Neither was the hospital, though so near. Shelters had been dug in the hills, into which most of the mobile patients were taken, but some of them hurried to the top of the hill instead, to watch the fray from that vantage point. On one occasion Rupert was horrified to learn that a woman whose cataract he had removed the previous day was one of these sightseers. But as she came to no harm, he wondered if the week of careful bed rest was really necessary.

It was in the autumn of 1941 that he was asked to go into the neighbouring province of Ningsia as the doctor with an evangelistic team. He set off happily enough down river on a large raft of ox skins on a wooden frame, which was carrying a cargo of wool. The journey took five days to Chungwei, where the medico-evangelistic campaign started.

It did not go well. Unlike most of the other places to which the missionary doctors went, the people of Chungwei were apparently not interested, either in the doctor or the evangelistic team. Then Rupert himself began to feel

unwell. He did not take it seriously at first, but
when he found that his efforts at self treatment
were having no effect he looked at himself in a
mirror and saw that the whites of his eyes were
turning yellow. Then he realized what was the
matter with him.

'So I took to my bed with what was then
called catarrhal jaundice, but which would now
be known as a form of hepatitis.' The bed he
took to was that of one of the missionaries in
Chungwei, and for a time Rupert did not know
or even care, what happened. He had never felt
so ill in his life. The Chungwei missionaries were
alarmed, particularly as the gate-keeper's wife
had just died of some sort of jaundice disease,
so they phoned through promptly to Mission
authorities, and action followed immediately. A
missionary nurse must be sent to look after him,
and instructions were issued for her to proceed
as quickly as possible to Chungwei.

When Rupert's blood bile level had come down
sufficiently for him to take notice of what was
happening around him, he realized that the
young woman who brought him his food, took
his temperature, and generally attended to him
was one whose picture he had seen some months
previously in the Mission's magazine. Jeannette
Barbour was her name, and she had written
briefly about herself. She had been born in
Rhodesia (Zimbabwe) but had trained as a nurse
in Edinburgh, and at the time of reading it Rupert
had thought that she sounded interesting.

By the time he was well enough to travel he
was convinced that she was the one whom, as

he put it, 'God had prepared for me.' He had been honest enough, even at the height of his emotional involvement with the nurse in Tite Street to admit to himself that he was not really sure that it was in God's plan for them to marry. There was no such doubt where Jeannette was concerned.

When he left Chungwei for a month's convalescence in Kinki, it involved a five mile bicycle ride to get to the river, and Jeannette accompanied him. He was used to cycling, and the machine he had was in good condition, but 'those five miles seemed very long, and my bicycle extraordinarily hard to push.' So the journey was not taken in a hurry. When they arrived at the river they found that the raft he was to travel on had been delayed, very conveniently prolonging their time alone together. 'So we went to the inn to rest and get something to eat, to find that the only food available was thick noodles swimming in mutton fat and burning with chillies – upon which highly unsuitable diet a rapid recovery started . . . !'

Perhaps the rapid recovery was partly to be attributed to the talk they were able to have, seated on rough wooden benches in view of the Muslim inn-keeper as he cooked their food in a pot over an open fire. At any rate, the recovery continued after his arrival at Kinki. He remained there with the Stanley Rowes for a month, mainly spent in language study, but during that time a long awaited letter from England was delivered. It had been written months before, but having merely been sent by surface, rather than by air mail, it had taken about ten weeks rather than ten days to arrive.

It was from the nurse in Tite Street. She readily agreed to Rupert's suggestion that perhaps it was not the Lord's will for her to marry him. So that was satisfactorily settled. He confided the situation to Norah Rowe – he wanted to talk privately to Jeannette.

Norah, mindful of Chinese etiquette, but eager to help the young couple, invited them both into her dining room, then quietly withdrew into an adjoining room – a chaperone ready at hand if needed. She had not been there long before she heard the front gate bang, and saw a visitor walking briskly towards the house. The chaperone acted quickly. There was a hasty change of position, and by the time the visitor entered Jeannette was in the next room, Norah was seated decorously on the settee, while Rupert was bending over his study books at the table. But when he cycled back to Lanchow, fully recovered from the effects of hepatitis, he was already quietly engaged to Jeannette.

4

Regions beyond

If Rupert's engagement had proceeded swiftly and smoothly, getting married proved no easy matter. First of all Jeannette had to complete her two years in China, and pass the necessary language exam to fulfil Mission requirements. The Second World War was at its height, with German armies still advancing in Europe, and the Japanese, not only in China, but beyond, invading the Philippines, Java, New Guinea . . . The Japanese attack on the US base in Pearl Harbour had brought the uneasy neutrality of the Allies in China to an end, and as far as the missionary body was concerned, it was cut in half. American, British, Australian nationals in the Japanese occupied territories were promptly interned for the duration of war, while those still in Free China were faced with increasing difficulties of communication with their home countries, and restrictions on financial support. So when, in the autumn of 1942, Jeannette had fulfilled the Mission's requirements, 'we hit a snag,' as Rupert put it. Where could they find in China's north-west someone qualified to perform the ceremony that would make them legally man and wife?

'There was no ordained Anglican clergyman, nor British consul nearer than Chungking, which was an expensive air journey away; and though we were assured by the Embassy that a wedding by some other ordained minister would be adequate for passport purposes, there was some doubt as to whether any offspring would be legitimate. So we decided we had better wait. By selling off possessions we eventually managed to collect enough money to pay for the return air tickets to Chungking, only to find the fares had doubled overnight.

'Needless to say, we prayed a lot about this problem.' The Mission authorities were not indifferent to the predicament, either, and eventually it was solved by the simple expedient of sending the Rev Gordon Aldis by air to Lanchow to perform the ceremony, thereby achieving the required result for the price of one air ticket instead of two.

The wedding itself was conducted in a manner familiar enough to the missionaries, with hymns and Bible reading and prayers providing the setting for the solemn act, in the presence of Almighty God, of mutual commitment 'until death parts us.' However, to the Chinese who were present it was different from anything they had been accustomed to. The bride was dressed in a new, but ordinary Chinese gown, there were no fire crackers, no extravagant feast – in fact, as one woman exclaimed with surprise, 'It was just

like a church service!' When the ceremony was
over and a simple reception held, in the home of
one of the missionaries, things happened just as
on Sunday. Everyone went home, or back to their
normal activities, while the bride and bridegroom
strolled off together after acknowledging smil-
ingly the congratulations of their friends. They
were going for a walk on the river, they said, and
set off down the narrow street to the bank. The
date was 14 January, 1943, and the Yellow River
was frozen. No coracles or rafts were needed to
cross to the opposite bank. They simply walked
across. They inspected the camels picketted on
the north bank, and saw the drinking holes that
had been dug out for them in the ice. 'Not quite
one's usual idea of camels in the desert!' They
chatted to the drivers, who told them they had
come from Mongolia, bringing wool for proces-
sing in the factory below the hospital. They
only travelled by night, the drivers explained to
avoid meeting motor vehicles, which were liable
to scatter the string across the Gobi desert.

'Then we returned to a lovely supper prepared
by David and Jessie Bentley-Taylor.' And there
was even a wedding cake. 'By this time many
goods were off the market, and our most valuable
wedding present was a 3lb bag of white sugar.
Normally sweetening was with saccharine, malt,
or buck-wheat honey, none of which made very
good cakes!'

After that they settled in the big Mission
compound in the city, where a small Chinese
style home had been prepared for them in what
was originally a stable. And so they commenced

married life. There was no way of having a honeymoon in the northwest in the depth of winter. That must wait until the weather got warmer. Instead, they went over to work in the hospital in the mornings and opened a clinic on the church premises in the afternoons, with Jeannette overseeing the nursing and also dispensing the medicines. They remained there for several weeks until a tragedy in the hospital brought them back to live there: the wife of Dr Stanley Hoyte died of typhus fever.

Dr Hoyte was already completely separated from his children, who were interned, along with the rest of the Chefoo school in Japanese occupied territory. It was out of the question for him to do anything else but remain where he was for the duration of the war – and who could tell how long that would be? So Rupert and Jeannette went to live with him, alleviating his loneliness, and incidentally relieving him of unaccustomed housekeeping responsibilities. It was not until seven months had passed that they eventually set off on their honeymoon.

'We had planned to take it in July, but it had poured with exceptional rain, and it was not until August that we were able to set out for Labrang on borrowed horses. We travelled by a circuitous route because of broken bridges and washed out roads, and were amazed to see the results of the heavy rain. We passed fields of wheat six feet high, and of barley eight feet high. Many of the stalks were bearing two or three ears of cereal, for with adequate water, and plenty of animal and human fertilizer the local soil produces excellent crops.'

They were reminded of Pharoah's dream, in which he saw stalks of corn bearing seven ears – 'maybe if we had searched diligently we might have found one!' Later on an old Muslim man leading a lamb up a small mountain was seen, and their guide told them there was a holy tree on top where people went to sacrifice, to obtain forgiveness of sins. There was something basic and primitive about the folk religion of animism in these vast, sparsely populated areas, different from the worship of many gods in the Chinese temples, or the prostrations of the Muslims in their mosques. They felt they were being transported back in time to the days of Genesis, and thought of Abraham slowly mounting the hill where he was prepared to sacrifice Isaac.

Although the place they were making for was Labrang, south of Lanchow, they decided to make a two day detour to visit the Gordon Bells in Hwalung. Their little son had had rheumatic fever, and Rupert wanted to find out for himself how the child was progressing. For Dorothy Bell the memory of that visit was fresh forty years afterwards, for it came at a time when she and her husband were feeling worn down by the isolation in which they were living, and anxiety about their child.

'The thoughtfulness of those two who took time out of their short holiday to help us was a very bright spot in those difficult days. It was good to chat with Jeannette Clarke that night. She was the first white woman I had seen in over a year.' And there was more to it than that, as was discovered the next day, for 'the place was mobbed with folks long before breakfast.

'Word had spread that the Jesus about whom the foreigners preached had come to town! Someone had recognized Rupert as the one who had performed the operations for cataract a few years earlier. It was a job even to clear a place for the doctor to work. In the afternoon the dining room table was requisitioned for one or two simple operations. The result of that day's work did not lessen the doctor's reputation.'

None of them had any inkling at the time that in this very place Rupert's reputation was to be called into question at a public trial. And that here he was to prove in new ways what was involved in being a good soldier of Jesus Christ. But in 1944 whatever might be happening in other parts of China, things were fairly peaceful up in the north-west, apart from local banditry and official skirmishes with Muslims, and after a couple of days Rupert and Jeannette moved on. They eventually reached their destination in the hospitable home of Christian and Missionary Alliance missionaries, who had invited them to stay.

Mr and Mrs Griebenow had been living in Labrang for a number of years, and their special concern was for the Tibetans. One of the largest and most important of the Tibetan lamaseries (monasteries), known as Kum Bum, was in the area, and here for the first time Rupert and Jeannette saw the pilgrims prostrating themselves full length on the ground, around its sacred precincts, heard the booming of the drums and the snorting sound of the long, curved horns, the incessant chanting of the lamas, and sensed the mesmeric power of a religion that had held the minds of men in bondage for centuries.

They saw another, and more attractive side of Tibetan life, too, as they were introduced to Tibetan people in their own countryside.

'It was the time when the sedentary Tibetans camped out whilst their houses were cleaned from the year's dirt and insects, and a new coat of white-wash applied. A time of cheerful feasting in their tents, very reminiscent of the Old Testament's Feast of Tabernacles. We were introduced to their staple diet of roasted barley flour and buttered tea, too. We could manage that well enough when fresh butter was used, but never enjoyed it when made with rancid butter, so highly esteemed by the local people.

'At the end of the month we were able to go home by a more direct route, over repaired bridges and tracks that had been made over the gullies. The Tibetan horse-boy took a poor view of us as we only rode twenty or thirty miles a day, whilst his mistress often rode forty or fifty. But when Jeannette asked him if she enjoyed it, he did admit that sometimes she cried!'

They returned to the familiar round of hospital work in Lanchow, but they had been made aware of a vast, untracked region beyond the crowded Chinese towns and villages, and of a bold-eyed, roistering, hardy people scattered thinly over it. Every now and then some of those people

found their way to the hospital, having travelled for days to get there – women with thick
black braided hair coiled round their heads, ear-
rings dangling, full skirts swirling round their
ankles; men in long boots and sheepskin gar-
ments, striding along the road by the river.
Rupert and Jeannette always noticed them, felt
drawn towards them. But the duties of the busy
hospital occupied their thoughts and dominated
their activities, though for Rupert there were
sometimes urgent calls to other districts.

On one occasion he went to Tienshui in the
south of the province to deal with the troublesome
tonsils of the missionaries' little boy. 'The tonsils
were duly removed upon the dining room table,
under a general anaesthetic which I induced, and
which was maintained by a missionary who had
had a little nursing training. The child made a
good recovery.' Some months later he was again
called to Tienshui, this time to attend to an aged
missionary who had been thrown from the top
of a truck on which he was travelling. Rupert's
outstanding memories of that visit were of the
first night, when his sleep was disturbed by the
incessant sound of rats, and the second, on which
he caught eight of them, one after the other, in
a trap that had to be reset each time. 'It is
said that rats will be very wary of the smell
of rat-blood, but the later victims must have
paddled through a large patch of it. Anyway,
the campaign was highly successful, and I had
no more broken nights.'

However, there was one journey which he had
to make about which he divulged very little

until years later. It was in December 1943, and there was the threat that the Japanese were planning to invade Ningsia province (now called Inner Mongolia). Mission authorities therefore instructed their missionaries to withdraw from the area, and as one of the missionaries was fairly advanced in pregnancy, Rupert was asked to go and meet them.

'And so, on 23 December at first light I set out on my Raleigh three-speed bicycle to meet the party. It was a beautiful sunny day, and in my sheepskin coat, fur hat, and several layers of woollens I was warm enough. On the carrier I had a change of clothing and a wadded quilt, and slung around the bike, or round my waist was a complete medical kit, including the wherewithal for a Caesarian section.

'I had never previously travelled the road, but was assured that all I had to do was to follow the telegraph wires and they would lead me to Chingyuan, the Kansu-Ningsia border city. But at about noon the road forked, and the wires followed neither! After cycling for about a couple of hours up a gentle hill I met the first pedestrian, who assured me that I had taken the wrong fork. So I had to return to the junction and start up a steep hill, which soon persuaded me to take off my sheepskin coat and tie that also to the carrier. Towards dusk, when I was pushing my bike, three tough-looking characters swung down the hill, whom I correctly diagnosed as bandits, but incorrectly supposed were 'off duty'. They caught up with me and forced me to stop – one of them had a revolver, one a knife, and one an odd weapon made from telegraph wire which did not look very dangerous – but I did not tempt him to try it out on me.'

All Rupert's relations, friends and even acquaintances would have agreed that he was unflappable. Whatever happened, it seemed that he never lost his head. The probability is that his three assailants, if questioned, would have come to the same conclusion. Their victim evidently took a philosophical view of his situation, accepting it without a struggle, and when they had tied him up with the rope from his carrier he watched them going through his luggage apparently dispassionately. Then he vouchsafed a remark.

'If you steal my bike you'll get caught,' he pointed out mildly. 'It's unique in the district – it would be recognised immediately.'

'That's all right,' they replied reassuringly. 'All we want is money.' Having relieved him of all that he had they discussed briefly whether they should kill him, but decided that it was unnecessary. They would merely tie his wrists behind his back – that would hold him up long enough for them to get well away.

Then he had something else to say. Wasn't it rather inhuman to leave him like that, without so much as the price of a bowl of noodles on him? The appeal to common humanity rarely fell on deaf ears in China, as he knew, 'So they agreed to give me enough money to buy a meal at the next inn, and then off they went.

'Rubbing the rope against a sharpish rock proved ineffective, and I managed to extract a pair of scissors from the surgical kit – which was quite a feat with wrists tied behind me! However, that just made holes in the sleeves of my pullover, and the rope proved much too tough for surgical scissors. Eventually I managed to wriggle free, to collect my belongings, and to look around for a cave in which to spend the night. In the Lord's goodness there was one not far away, and there I settled down in my sheepskin coat, wadded boots and wadded quilt, and managed to get some sleep, despite the extreme cold, fortified by some chunks of fudge with which my wife had supplied me for Christmas.

'As soon as it was light I pushed on up the hill, and found that the pass was only about a quarter of a mile away, after which I coasted down about ten miles to a hamlet where there was an inn which supplied me with some very welcome hot noodles. By noon of Christmas Eve I had reached Chingyuan.'

The most natural thing in such circumstances would have been to relate his experiences to the three women missionaries there, but Rupert had already made up his mind that he would keep quiet about the whole affair. Jeannette must not hear about it. It would upset her, and make her anxious every time he had to set out on a similar sort of journey. He therefore concentrated on passing on news about Lanchow, what was known about the progress of the war, surmising when the party travelling towards them was likely to arrive — anything rather than what had happened to him during the last thirty-six hours.

'However, when the two young ones had gone

to bed I was able to unburden myself to Faith Leewenberg, who was an old friend, and from whom I was able to borrow some money to cover road expenses.

'It was still sunny on Christmas day, though very cold, and I made good progress on a fairly good dirt road, lunched on the sandwiches kindly provided, and just before dusk reached the inn where I planned to pass the night. But alas, as on a far more important Christmas day, it was a case of there being no room in the inn, which was packed with muleteers and their animals. However, the inn-keeper assured me that it was only ten miles on to the city, and that the moon was almost full.

'And so I started off again – and very shortly entered a narrow valley just ideal for ambush by robbers. (It was not only the last month in the western calendar but also in the lunar calendar, and in that month everybody has to repay their debts – so no sensible person ventures on the road at dusk!) My plan was to rush through it, but straightaway I hit a sharp rock and burst the back tyre . . .

'Never had I done such a quick repair! It was not a very air-tight one, and needed re-pumping about every mile or so. Those ten miles took a long time to cover. However, the city was reached at about ten o'clock and I was soon receiving a warm welcome from the Stanley Rowes, in whose home I had become engaged two years before. The following evening the evacuees arrived, and in due course we all set off for Lanchow at a decorous speed, arriving there in

comparative safety and comfort, with gratitude
for the Lord's keeping power – and, incidentally, for the fact that I had not accepted the
loan of a pistol which a friendly official had
pressed on me!'

5

The vision that materialised

As the limousines containing the Russian diplomats swept off down the main road in Lanchow, Rupert and his companions turned into the side street leading to the Mission compound. 'The proletariat slogging it through the mud,' he observed drily, and the others chuckled. The Party members certainly seemed to have things easier, they agreed, as they trudged home. Plenty of money for tobacco, too. The place had been filled with smoke from their pipes, as they sat around the V-shaped table.

They had all been to a ceremony to celebrate the successful conclusion in Europe of World War Two; and a few months later the dropping of the atomic bomb on Hiroshima heralded the sudden end of the war in the Far East. International events were moving fast. The Cold War between the USSR and her erstwhile allies started, with Germany cut in half, and the Berlin Wall like a deadly wound plunged through the heart of the capital. And in China the brittle understanding that had held together the Communist inspired guerillas and the Nationalists in resistance against the invading Japanese was rapidly snapping. The leaders of the celebrated Long March had been biding their time in the mountains of the north, but now they were prepared to make their bid for power.

As far as the missionaries in Lanchow were concerned, these events were too remote for most of them to worry about. Their sights were set in other directions, and for Rupert and Jeannette, interest in the Tibetans was becoming a deep conviction that something more ought to be done for them.

'We were receiving more and more Tibetans in the Lanchow hospital, and as they had to come at least a week's journey to us, on foot or on yaks, we felt it would be a very good thing if we could start some medical work in their own territory. At the same time, our American friends in the Christian and Missionary Alliance felt they were not being at all successful in reaching the Tibetans with the Gospel. They earnestly persuaded us to consider such a project, to soften the Tibetans by a practical demonstration of the love of Christ. But as we had no spare nurses, doctors, medicines or surgical instruments there was little hope of starting such a work in the near future.'

But the thought remained, though life in Lanchow went on as usual – and sometimes not as usual, for during a severe epidemic of typhoid fever and cholera, against which he had been vaccinated four times, Rupert himself became a victim.

'One day I felt exceedingly chilly, despite my

sheepskin coat and woollens, so I lay down
in a patch of sunshine on the verandah until
Jeannette came home and put me to bed. Thereafter I have only vague memories of fever,
headaches, and being persuaded to take doses
of horrible tasting sedatives of bromide and
chloral, so that I suppose I must have had rowdy
tendencies. After ten days the fever abated and
I gradually recovered, so we went up to a hill
bungalow with several donkey loads of coal as
well as supplies for a fortnight. Milk and goats's
meat we were able to obtain by barter of clothing,
and further supplies, mail and local news arrived
by occasional visits of the hospital donkey.

'Late in 1946 we went back to Britain for
furlough.'

The Britain to which they returned seemed
bleak and cold, with bomb sites revealing something of the battering its cities had taken during
the war. Food was still rationed, and coupons as
well as cash were required to buy clothes. All the
same, in the Church there was a resurgence of
life, and in some circles interest was being especially focussed on Tibet. Organisations that had
previously not worked on its borders were moving
towards the closed lands of central Asia, and to
reach 'the roof of the world' with the Gospel of
Jesus Christ was the avowed aim of ardent young
people, some of whom were to prove, in the years
ahead, the sincerity of their dedication. When
Rupert had the opportunity to speak about his
desire to start a medical work on the Tibetan
border of north-west China, he was encouraged
by many people assuring him of their prayers.

However, apart from that he admitted that he found post-war Britain underheated and dismal, and was delighted when a passage was arranged for him and Jeannette to go to her parents in South Africa.

'There was an eighteen-month waiting list for passages in England, but one of our Norwegian associates was able to book a couple of unwanted berths from Norway, which we picked up at Southampton. We spent several happy, sunny months in Johannesburg before returning to China, and as we had a few days between ships in Colombo, it was possible to make a quick trip to see Miss Amy Carmichael and the lovely work of the Dohnavur Fellowship in South India before proceeding onwards to China.'

From the missionary point of view, China was enjoying a halcyon period. With the Generalissimo an avowed Christian, doors that normally would have been hard to enter were wide open. The Pocket Testament League was holding meetings and distributing Scriptures freely in the armed forces. Evangelists were going into prisons, in the universities groups of students were being gathered to form Christian fellowships, while evangelistic campaigns could be organized without any interference from officials, in both town and country.

What was even more encouraging for the long-sighted was the strength and vitality of the Chinese Church as a whole, as evidenced in the growth of indigenous movements and spiritual leaders, revealed in various ways. In north Shantung the Jesus Family had established its

communal centre, in Peking Wang Ming Tao
was preaching to a congregation that was too
great for the building to hold, and starting his
widespread writing ministry, while farther south
the Little Flock with Watchman Nee as its leader,
was spreading out from Shanghai to towns and
cities in neighbouring provinces. And groups of
believers were emerging who were conscious of
a divine urge to take the Gospel to tribes and
races on the borders of their land. It was through
one of these that Rupert and Jeannette began to
see on their arrival back in China the answer to
their prayers that they might move out to work
among Tibetans.

'Arriving at Mission Headquarters in Shanghai, we were speedily summoned to meet the
Director for the north-west region, who enquired
whether we would be willing to open a clinic for
Tibetans on the border! And so we discovered
that our prayers had been answered by the
formation of a Chinese Christian organisation
called the Holy Light Rural Medical Service.
This organisation had access to large supplies of
ex-US military medical supplies which had been
handed over to a Chinese branch of the United
Nations Organisation, and they promised that
they would fly out a Chinese doctor and four
nurses from the city of Kaifeng in Henan, which
was surrounded by Communist troops.'

And so the vision became a reality. It was
decided that the clinic should be opened in
Hwalung, where Rupert was already known,
and where the Mission had property. A New
Zealand couple, Norman and Amy Macintosh

went ahead to prepare for the medical team, and
they not only saw to the necessary maintenance
work on the property, but started investigating
the whole area around Hwalung, especially in
regard to the Tibetan population. There were
some sixty lamaseries in the Hwalung-Kweiteh
area and they were dismayed at what they saw
of conditions in some of them – little boys taken
early in life to become lamas, and learning to
indulge in the vices of homosexuality, promis-
cuity and gambling, as well as the worship and
invoking of spirits. Every Tibetan family sent
at least one son to become a lama – it was
estimated that practically a quarter of the male
population was to be found in the lamaseries.
The Tibetans themselves, the sedentary and
the nomads, accepted without question the rule
of the lamas. A friendly, outgoing people the
Macintoshes found them, but strangely imper-
vious to the solemn facts of judgment before the
throne of a Holy God, and forgiveness through
faith in Christ.

Six weeks after the Macintoshes had settled
into the Mission property in Hwalung the medical team arrived, and Rupert reported,

'By 4 July 1948 we were ready to open the
clinic, but as the clinic nurse, Ruth Duncan,
was from Texas we decided that Independence
Day must first be celebrated, and the official
opening was on 5 July. At first it was just a
clinic, with Norman and Amy Macintosh looking after maintenance and preaching* and with

* See *Never Say Can't* by Linnet Hinton.

Ruth Duncan over-seeing the nursing. One missionary doctor went up from Lanchow every two
months, and the Chinese doctor, Dr Lee and two
Chinese nurses also rotated between Lanchow
and Hwalung. (To their 'down-country' eyes it
seemed a very cold, barren and unfriendly part
of the world, populated largely by Muslims and
Tibetans antagonistic to the Han Chinese!)

'Hwalung is about the size of Trafalgar Square,
10,000 feet above sea level, with snow every
month except August, and the ground is frozen
for eight months of the year, so that only barley, rape and Chinese cabbage could be grown
locally. All other food had to be imported from
warmer regions, as well as donkey-loads of coal
and wood. However, the climate was bracing and
healthy, and one soon became accustomed to the
rarefied atmosphere – unless one tried to push-
start the jeep . . .

'We usually managed the journey from Lanchow
in two days when the roads and the jeep were in
reasonable repair, but on one occasion the fuel
pump failed.'

In such circumstances Rupert's ingenuity flourished. He had already made a name for himself among the hospital staff in Lanchow along
this line, during the war, when no surgical or
any other equipment could get through. Rupert
always seemed to find a satisfactory substitute,
even when a fellow missionary was thrown over
the handle-bars of his bicycle and fractured his
jaw. He wired the fracture by using part of a
thermos spring, and everyone said that Eric was
much better-looking afterwards! So when the fuel

pump of the jeep failed, Rupert stood thinking for a minute or two, then opened his medical box. He had the solution.

'So we completed the journey with me holding a petrol can on the roof, and the fuel running down to the engine through my stethoscope tubing. However, the two-monthly exchange of doctors was not very satisfactory for the clinic, and it was far from popular with the doctors' wives.

'So Jeannette and I thought and prayed about permanently leaving the comparative comfort of Lanchow, and moving up to Hwalung. As the days went by we became more and more sure that it was the right thing to do, and the plan was approved by the hospital missionaries, and by headquarters in Shanghai. We felt it to be God's will for us, and perhaps as a bonus, God sent Jeannette her first pregnancy after six years of married life.

'Once settled in Hwalung we set about turning the clinic into a hospital, and with the aid of four local ward orderlies who could speak both Chinese and Tibetan, we were able to start surgery in earnest. Tibetans came in good numbers – a few on horseback, mostly on yaks or walking, and many of them suffering from hydatid cysts of the liver or other organs. These are caused by a small tape-worm which normally lives in sheep, and which is transmitted to humans by the dogs which shared their tents. They started as small as a pea, but could grow to the size of a full-term pregnancy, largely destroying the liver. But they could almost all be cured by operation under local anaesthesia. The extraction of the jelly-like cyst lining was always a moment of triumph for the family members witnessing the operation.'

There was no question of operations being conducted in the strict privacy of the operating theatre – it was understood that close relatives, at any rate, should see what went on. On one occasion a delighted family member placed an extra two silver dollars on the operating sheet to show his gratification, produced from the depths of his filthy sheepskin gown in unconscious defiance of the most elementary laws of hygiene. The imperturbable Rupert carried on through it all, even taking part in conversations when called upon to do so. He was actually in the middle of performing a delicate operation one day when a messenger appeared to announce that a big convoy of Tibetan patients was on the way.

'It proved to be the biggest rush we had. An immensely fat old Living Buddha had brought along fifty-odd of his nomads as patients. Forty-six of them required operations, and we had only a twenty bed hospital, and that was already fairly full. And they stated that they must all be fit to travel back their twenty-eight day's journey in three weeks time . . .

'Well, somehow or other we managed to get them all worked off in ten days or so. Surgery had to be planned according to the estimated time for recovery, and we started operating after lunch each day, usually finishing by the early morning. About a dozen of them had cataracts, and about a dozen needed an internal urethrotomy for urethral stricture (the Tibetans are riddled with syphilis and gonorrhea and all sorts of venereal diseases you don't see at home). Then about another dozen had hydatid cysts of the liver (very common amongst them) and the remaining dozen odds and ends – sterine fibroids, ovarian cysts, etc. The leader of the convoy was a 'Living Buddha', believed to be a reincarnation of the Buddha, but he was so vastly obese that we decided that there was no way whereby we could get him to and from the operating theatre, and so his cataract was removed in his own bed, by the light of a kerosene pressure-lamp, and he made a good recovery.

'So what with one thing and the other, we were kept pretty much on the hop, especially as our "operating theatre" was our dispensary-dressing-room in the mornings. It was a time for very hard work, but at the end of the three weeks they were all fit to travel, and started off on their four week journey home. I think that if they had been able to travel direct they would have had a much shorter journey, but they had to travel by a circuitous route to avoid a hostile clan.'

The fame of the foreign doctor in Hwalung who worked miracles was spreading among the Tibetans further up in the barren mountains where they roamed at will, free from the unwelcome presence of the Chinese. This foreign doctor was good to the Tibetans, treated them just as well as he treated the Chinese! A few months later a delegation arrived at the hospital with an urgent invitation for him to move into their territory, where they promised to provide buildings and everything he might require.

How readily he would have responded! All the

patients who had been in the hospital had heard
the Gospel, most of them for the first time, and
had taken New Testaments or Gospel portions
home with them. The practical demonstration,
through medical assistance, of the compassion
of Christ had proved effective. But the invitation
came too late. The door that had seemed to be
opening began relentlessly to close.

The civil war in China was over. The Communist regiments emerging from the northern
province where they had been entranched during
the war against the invading Japanese, proved
too strong for the weakened Nationalists. Well
disciplined and well fed, they encountered little
opposition, and by September 1949 General Mao
Tse-Tung had proclaimed in Beijing the estab-
lishment of the People's Republic of China. After
that the mopping up process proceeded fairly rapidly, the pattern of events in all places taking a
similar form. The Communist soldiers behaved
well, paying for what they bought, returning any
utensils they may have borrowed, in marked contrast to the Nationalist soldiers, under-paid and
under-fed, who all too often made off with anything they could lay hands on. The Communists
frequently gave a helping hand to the labourers,
and assured everyone that things would go on
just as usual and were getting better all the
time. A new element of happiness was introduced by entertainments in the streets, soldiers
appearing in some places in long flowing gowns
as they walked about on stilts, to the admira-
tion and amazement of all who liked that sort
of thing. Rousing songs of the revolution were

accompanied by an animated form of dancing with scarf-waving, which immediately attracted the young.

Not until the civil authorities came along and took control did things begin to look more ominous, with the calling of political meetings when the poor were urged to demand their rights, to bring to justice the rich who had exploited them, voice their complaints against officials who had deceived them, and expose the supporters of the imperialistic Nationalist Government.

Then the accusation meetings started, when the wealthy landowners, the prominent officials, the people who were suspected of dealings with the imperialistic West were brought to trial. The prisoners, roped or chained, were made to kneel on the platforms erected in public places, while the people were called upon to pass judgment. The more severe the judgment, the better, so . . .

'Confiscate all his property! Send him to labour camp! Execute him!' And woe betide those who didn't shout, those who displayed any sort of sympathy with the accused. They could expect to be arrested later – probably at night.

Although there had been some heavy fighting in the Lanchow area, the take-over in Hwalung had been fairly peaceful, with only the local Muslim troops resisting 'the liberating army.' Work in the hospital continued with very little interference from the new authorities, and from Rupert's point of view the outstanding event of the year was a very personal one. He became a father.

'On Christmas Eve baby Humphrey was delivered, weighing less than four pounds (which was the lowest weight our scales would show.) His low weight was probably due to the oxygen-poor atmosphere of lofty Hwalung, but despite a strangulated hernia when one month old (which I had to repair under local anaesthesia) he put on weight steadily – in fact, he was such a determined suckler that he often had indigestion.' It was a frequent sight to see Jeannette with a squealing baby in one arm, while with her free hand she was diligently preparing saline solution for intravenous use in the hospital. She took a full share in the work – had done so from the start, when the clinic was first opened, and within a week upward of four hundred patients had received treatment. In those early days there were no beds, just straw filled mattresses on the floor, although later wooden beds were made, which made things easier for the nursing staff, even if the patients, most of them Tibetan, were unimpressed by the improvement. Their family attendants slept in bunk beds at the end of the ward, making their relative's food and generally looking after them. Any other members of patients' families who happened to be around slept in a large room where there was a huge mud brick bed which was heated from below. In this room the Tibetans did their cooking on open fires of dried yak dung, which admittedly made the place smoky and sooty, but there were times when the wards were so full that patients had to be accommodated here – there was nowhere else to put them.

'This was the cause of a major row when a Communist soldier was admitted with "gas-gangrene". I had no ward-bed available – and anyhow I was not keen to admit this highly infectious case into the ward. Fortunately the army was able to provide me with plenty of penicillin and he made a good recovery after surgery. But to have placed this "people's hero" in that sooty room was infuriating to the authorities. I am afraid that I "blew my top", and told them that poor as our effort might be, we were actually doing something to help the Tibetans – which was more than any Han-Chinese government had ever done. The affair simmered down, but as James says in his epistle, "The wrath of man does not work the righteousness of God." Doubtless it was a good reason for making trouble for me later.'

6

Closing doors

Two armed soldiers were walking around the hospital compound, looking rather contemptuously in the wards, the dispensary, the store rooms. No-one tried to stop them. The gatekeeper had stood politely aside when they marched in, the patients and their family attendants backed away as they passed by, and Jeannette quietly went on with what she was doing – until she saw them enter the small room where Karen Hemmingby was lying in bed with her newborn baby.

Karen Hemmingby and her husband were members of the Norwegian Pentecostal Mission, and had come from their mission station two or three days' journey further in Tibetan territory for the birth of their third child. It had not been an easy delivery, and as Arne Hemmingby wrote about it forty years later, it was still fresh in his memory. He wrote,

'Most of us foreigners at the hospital were more or less anxious and active around Dr Clarke and the mother. Really, we felt thankful for

Dr Clarke's proficiency in obstetric aid, in that wilderness.

'A few days after the delivery, the mother with the newborn baby still in bed, they got an unexpected and undesirable visit. Two armed soldiers entered their room.

'As it happened, Mrs Clarke (Jeannette) observed them, and as she knew very well that this was far from good Chinese conduct, even for soldiers, she just entered the room as well, and asked the armed men to be so kind as to leave the mother and child alone. This quickly developed into a most critical situation. The angry and hot-headed men levelled their guns at Mrs Clarke, and as she bravely protested against their behaviour, the atmosphere became still more tense.

'Then, at the identical moment, Dr Clarke quietly entered the scene. In the following few minutes some of his strong and wise personality was clearly revealed. With his well-spoken Chinese in a polite and sedate way he turned the situation . . . the violent emotions sank considerably as Dr Clarke suggested that he might go to the military headquarters for further talks. So Mrs Clarke was left in peace.'

Although there were no immediate repercussions from this incident, it gave an indication of the way the situation under Communist rule was likely to develop. And there were other even more serious indications of the effect it would have. The numbers of people attending services in the church, never large, were dwindling noticeably. It was the same in other places. From all over

the country similar reports were reaching the
CIM headquarters in Shanghai, and the reason
was evident. Communist officials were accusing
those associating with the missionaries of being
'running dogs of the Imperialist nations' and the
Christians who were loyal to them were having a
bad time. The fact had to be faced that missionaries were no longer a help to the Church, but a
hindrance.

'Our presence is making things worse for the
very people we most want to help,' was the
expressed view of HQ staff. 'The sooner we get
out, the better.' And the day came in December
1950 when the decision was taken. After eighty-
five years in China, the China Inland Mission
was to withdraw – completely.

So Rupert, along with several hundred other
members of the Mission scattered over China,
received his instructions. He was to close the
hospital and proceed with his wife and child and
fellow workers, as soon as possible, to Sining, and
from there, in due course, to the British Crown
Colony of Hong Kong.

It was easier said than done, as those at Headquarters soon discovered. The new Government,
still pursuing its policy of eliminating the officials
connected with the Nationalists, the wealthy
landlords and the intelligentsia, was bringing
pressure on expatriates from the western nations
who still remained in China. Foreigners were
severely restricted regarding travel. They could
not move away anywhere without official permission to do so. As for getting out of China, to pass
through its barriers they must have exit visas.

And to obtain their exit visas, it must be proved that they had paid all their debts, that they had committed no crimes, and that they all had Chinese citizens prepared to vouch for them.

On the face of it, it looked simple enough until the Foreign Affairs Bureau, preserving an enigmatic silence, refused the Mission permission to advertise in the local paper announcing departures – the preliminary to application for an exit visa. The advertisement gave anyone who had a complaint to make the time to do it. Missionaries here and there were harassed, visited at night by police demanding to search premises, taken off for long periods of questioning, and required to fill in forms giving detailed summaries of their movements from birth. Funds were frozen. The situation was becoming quite sinister, like being involved in a war of nerves. Three months after the historic decision had been taken to withdraw the entire Mission from China, half of its members were still there, and unable to move.

'Unable to move' certainly summarised the situation in which the missionaries in Hwalung found themselves. There were six of them, the Rupert Clarkes, the Hemmingbys, Ruth Duncan from Texas and Ruth Gaardlas from Norway. The Macintoshes had moved some time before to open work among the Tibetans in Kweiteh. Application had been made to set in motion the formalities necessary to obtain exit visas, and in a visit to the Communist headquarters the official there had proved, in Rupert's words, 'not too unfriendly.' His instructions were that they should close the hospital forthwith, and prepare to leave the country. They could sell their personal belongings (not anything from the hospital) to pay their way to the coast. Meanwhile, he would apply to the provincial capital for their exit visas. It would take about two weeks, he said.

Five months later they were still waiting . . .

As Arne Hemmingby admitted, it was a time of suspense and tension. 'Then, suddenly, one Thursday in June, four soldiers entered the compound and commanded Dr Clarke and me to go with them.

'According to a rumour which had found its way into the compound, we thought it quite likely that we were to be put in prison. Consequently we started to talk about having some warm clothes with us, but our conversation came to an abrupt end by a harsh 'Shut up!' from the soldiers. And they led us, not to a prison, but to the headquarters, and into a hall where Dr Clarke and I had to stand between two long rows of armed guards. Then one of the four important-looking men in front of us told us what bad people we were, and how they planned to get rid of us. This was another situation in which the fine personality of Dr Clarke was revealed, to my encouragement.

'We were told that we had to leave two days later for Sining – a journey which would take at least four days. However, we were told to get there in three days. After that rather stressing experience we were permitted to return to the hospital compound.

'The following day the rain was pouring down,

and we wondered how we would get to Sining on the slippery roads. Dr Clarke contacted the guard at the gate, and asked,

' "As we have to leave for Sining tomorrow, may I go out to try to hire some mules?" "No, you just stay here", was the answer.

' "In that case, would you please help me with this problem?"

' "It's no affair of mine!"

' "Then how can we get away?"

' "You walk . . ."

' "But – what about the babies?"

' "You can carry them!"

'The rain continued to pour down, and we continued to prepare for the travelling – and to pray.'

That evening soldiers again arrived and took the two men to headquarters. They must receive written permission to leave Hwalung, they were told. After standing outside the office for an hour they were finally given the papers, and to their surprise no guard of soldiers accompanied them, only a blue-uniformed clerk. Halfway back to the hospital compound they met the man who had been carrying water for them, and again to their surprise the clerk accompanying them gave them permission to speak to him. Could he help them to get some sort of transport to take their party to Sining?

'About half an hour later we got a surprising answer from our water-carrier – and surely an answer to prayer! Some men from Sining had arrived with four coal-laden carts, drawn by small pony-like horses. They planned to return the following day, and would be very happy not to go with empty carts!'

A thankful but busy evening, rearranging luggage and preparing for the journey, a few hours sleep, then . . .

'We awoke to a most dramatic day. The men from Sining soon appeared with their empty carts, and we counted on a speedy departure. But as high officials and soldiers invaded the compound, we were stopped several times. "Not yet", they said.

'Then suddenly we experienced the tragedy – so deep in its sadness – which branded and dominated the last moments of our stay in Hwalung. A man who had been a co-worker at the hospital appeared, went up in front of Dr Clarke and accused him: "You have purposely killed some of your patients! You have . . ."

'Dr Clarke was standing there, quiet, silent, but firm and surely confident in God. He was not permitted to leave, but Mrs Clarke with Humphrey was forced to.

'One of the very last things that I clearly remember is that Dr Clarke laid his arm on Mrs Clarke's shoulder and said, "Now, you be brave, my dear." And brave she was!

'Thus we left together.' Rupert walked back alone into the compound.

When it was eventually cleared of the soldiers and the police, the onlookers and even the man who had accused him, he was left to take stock of his situation. His lot was not improved by the discovery that the carters had managed to steal about half his supply of money which, in the excitement of the moment, he had left in view. He realized that he would have to depend on what cash he had to pay the water-carrier, to buy food, postage stamps anything he might need. He would not be allowed to go to market, that was certain – so how was he to keep in touch with the outside world?

Meanwhile there was the practical consideration of where his next meal was to come from. The police had locked the hospital and the store rooms – 'This property belongs to the people,' he was given to understand. But he still had access to the deserted kitchens of the two nurses and the Hemmingby family, so he retrieved what he could find there – rice, potatoes, salt, flour, a few vegetables. Plenty of tea. He was glad of that . . .

It was strange to be walking around alone in the courtyards where for months there had been six adults and four children, including his own little 'Humpty'. He wondered how long he would be left there, and what the next move would be. Four days later he knew. It started with what had become the familiar noise of people in the drill ground close to the hospital. That was the place where the public trials were held, sometimes followed by the sharp sound of rifle shots, as prisoners were executed.

'I waited for four days, then heard a great deal of noise on the drill ground close to the hospital; then a Chinese Christian woman slipped in to tell me that I would be put up for a "people's trial" that afternoon. She told me to admit everything alleged against me, which was called "bowing to the will of the people." If I denied anything, that would be "resisting the will of the people", and would make for trouble.

'I was very grateful for her courage in coming to warn me, but considerably worried as to what I should do. I was sure that they would bring false charges, and to admit these would be lying. On the other hand, to deny them might make for serious repercussions.'

It was one of the few occasions when Rupert was really worried. He could not make up his mind what to do – it was in a turmoil. His mental faculties were no longer under his control, it seemed, and it was at this point that one of the promises of God suddenly steadied him. Words came quietly flooding into his mind as powerful and convincing as when spoken by Jesus to His followers nearly two thousand years before. 'And when they bring you before rulers and authorities, do not be anxious what you are to say, for the Holy Spirit will teach you in that very hour what you ought to say.'

He had read it many times before, the comforting exhortation not to worry or premeditate or think of what would be the best things to say – because when the time came the Holy Spirit Himself would give the right words. Now he had to act on it. So standing there alone in the empty room he prayed, committing the matter to the Lord, and then, in his practical way, stopped worrying.

'I spent the time much more profitably by filling my underclothes with DDT powder, in case I landed up in prison!' It proved to be a wise precaution.

'Early in the afternoon the police came along to collect me, and I was taken to the small City Hall, into which they had packed about two hundred people, who had to attend, willy-nilly. There the Commissar read out all sorts of charges against me, though the only one which could be proved was that some of the patients upon whom I had operated had later died – this, of course, was quite true, but scarcely proved that I was a member of the American CIA, which seemed to be what they were trying to prove. It was the time of the Korean war, when America was more unpopular with them than usual.

'After about four hours, in which the Lord had certainly given me the words to speak (all in Chinese), and in which I had been allowed to make a defence, the Commissar summed up my "wickedness" and demanded a verdict from the people.'

It was at this point that something went wrong. The time had come for the angry roar of voices, the vociferous demands for imprisonment or death. But instead, the crowd just stood silent. Again the Commissar shouted, demanding that they should give their verdict. Silence.

The officials were in a difficult position. There was a hurried consultation, then the Commissar adopted a different tactic. He pointed to the man who was known as the leader in the little church in Hwalung, and asked, 'What do you think ought to be done to him?'

Perhaps Rupert was not the only one who had prayed that day. Perhaps the few Christians who had been summoned to the trial had prayed that *they* might be given the right words to speak, that they might be spared either betraying the foreign doctor they knew so well, or adopting an attitude that would antagonise the authorities. At any rate, as Rupert listened to the man's answer, he applauded inwardly.

'I think he ought to be heavily fined and sent back to his own country,' was what he heard, and nothing could have pleased him better. He knew there was plenty of money in the bank at Shanghai to pay a fine, and he would be delighted to be returned to his own country! But the Commissar was not satisfied. He pointed next to the Muslim assistant mayor, who replied that he thought the accused should be sent to prison. Finally the Commissar got what he wanted, by pointing to the Chinese mayor, who shouted out,

'Kill him!'

It was a tense moment. As Rupert himself admitted, 'I did not think they really intended to kill me, but such suggestions in a Communist court are very unpleasant, and I was relieved when the Commissar said that he would put me in prison for the time being, and await instructions from the capital.' So to prison he went, like a common criminal, and was pushed into a cell about twenty feet by fifteen feet.

'And there were forty of us in it – mostly Muslims. There was just room to squat on the floor, but none to lie down or stretch one's legs. I was graciously granted a place against a wall by the cell commander, who was a disgraced soldier, but most of the prisoners just sat back to back. Some of them were handcuffed, either in front or behind, and some wore ankle shackles also. Twice a day we were allowed out to a meal of bread and water, and I was grateful to a fellow prisoner who told me to stow the bread in my shirt and concentrate on drinking as much water as possible. Twice a day we were also allowed out for toilet purposes at a stinking open pit. Otherwise we just sat, or tried to sleep, and I was very grateful for the DDT powder, as many of the prisoners had not had a decent wash in half a year

'My pocket Testament had been removed from me, but I could hum hymns to myself – only to find that the only one which I could remember completely was "The Lord's my Shepherd, I'll not want." However, that was a good one to hum. Then, after a few days, I suddenly remembered that it was 5 July – the third anniversary of the opening of the clinic!'

An anniversary! Anniversaries should be celebrated, but there was nothing he could do about it, so he asked the Lord to do something as a celebration instead. And that prayer was answered with heart-warming promptitude.

'Quite early the Commissar sent for me, and was quite polite, almost apologised for imprisoning me, saying that he had to do it to show that the People's Government was not afraid of foreigners. He then sent me back to the hospital compound under "house arrest", which meant that I might not leave the compound, nor might anyone enter, except for an old man who was instructed to buy food for me. As he was an opium addict, my food became a bit expensive!

'For the first few days I was allowed to receive mail, but on the same day that a telegram arrived to say that Jeannette had a booking on a ship to South Africa (so she was safe, anyway!) there also arrived a well-meant telegram from the British Charge d'Affaire in Peking, enquiring of my welfare, which probably convinced the officials that I was some sort of an agent. And so my mail was stopped.'

Nine months later Mission authorities reported that there were still sixteen members of the Mission who had so far been unable to get out of China. However, all of them could be accounted for, except one.

Nothing had been heard of Dr Rupert Clarke for eight months, and all letters and cables sent to him had remained unanswered.

7

Housebound

Rupert had drunk his morning cup of tea and was settling down to the next item in the daily programme he had planned for himself. The habits of discipline observed and learned in his childhood were standing him in good stead now. Not for nothing did he come of soldier stock, with daily drilling in peacetime as well as in war. And he knew the value of occupation for mind as well as body. First things must come first, he always decided, and the early hours of his lonely days were spent in Bible reading and prayer. Then came a breakfast of bread and tea, to be followed by any cleaning or mending that needed to be done.

After that was the time for a three mile walk. He knew exactly how many times he must stride round the courtyard to accomplish that. Once a week he did ten miles instead of three, to keep himself in trim for the time that would surely come when he would have to walk to Sining, en route eventually for Hong Kong and freedom. He intended to be physically ready for it.

This exercise over, it was time for study. He had nothing but his Bible and an old commentary on John's gospel until the official in charge was persuaded to allow him the loan of an impounded American text book of medicine. 'Through this vast tome I ploughed steadily, skipping only the pages about electrocardiograms, from which I had always shied away. I am not sure that I actually learned anything, but at any rate it was a good method of passing the time.'

The main meal of the day followed, usually noodles or boiled dumplings, if he had anything to put inside them. 'And so to bed,' with a novel to occupy his mind until sleep came.

It was as healthy a routine as he could devise in the circumstances, but there were times when the days seemed very long and weary, and he wondered when, and how, they would end. He was thankful that Jeannette and Humphrey were safely in sunny South Africa, and longed to join them. The thought sometimes occurred to him that he might try to escape across Tibet. He knew he would find good friends there on whom he could count for help. But reason told him that he was not equipped for the bitterly cold weather and snow-clad mountains, and that with his western face he would be too easily recognised – and that re-capture by the Communists would have very unpleasant consequences.

'Not having a very vivid imagination I did not often consider execution, and comforted myself that their usual method of dispatch was by a bullet through the base of the neck, which was messy but probably painless. Usually I pictured the scene as being with the ward orderly who was already imprisoned, and decided that we would recite the Lord's prayer, for the benefit of the assembled audience.' It would be the best way he could think of to die in those circumstances. But he dismissed the idea of trying to escape across Tibet, and with it the probability of capture, and turned his thoughts in another direction.

He wondered if he should lay down a 'prayer barrage' as he termed it, pleading incessantly for a speedy deliverance. This thought was in his mind when, having drunk his early morning tea, he settled to his Bible reading one day. He had come to Psalm 106, and was suddenly arrested by the words,

> . . . they lusted exceedingly in the wilderness, and tempted God in the desert. And He gave them their request, but sent leanness into their souls.

They obtained that for which they were yearning, pleading, demanding – but it brought them no satisfaction, rather the reverse. He was reminded of something Jeannette's mother once told her. She had been a missionary in South America for a time, and their leader had fallen ill. 'But the missionaries kept up a "prayer barrage", demanding that God should heal him. In the outcome, that good man did recover, but was such a changed character that he had to be expelled from the field!'

So Rupert decided against a 'prayer barrage' too. Instead, he would act on the exhortation to trust in the Lord, and wait patiently for Him, living as normally as possible in the loneliness and confinement of the hospital compound. He was glad of the little supply of novels that helped to wile away the evening hours – two or three by John Buchan, which he read about five times, two by Walter Scott, which he read ten times. 'But the one which I found best of all was Mrs Henry Wood's *"East Lynne"*, which is a very melodramatic Victorian story, but so well written that I enjoyed reading it more than fifteen times.'

Apart from the old man who carried in water and food, paid for by his steadily diminishing supply of cash, Rupert saw practically no-one. Occasionally he was visited by the police secretary, sometimes accompanied by a couple of policemen, but quite often alone, and when that happened Rupert knew what to expect. He had not come on a duty call, to deliver a Party line harangue. 'He was on a foraging expedition into the hospital stores, and I would attach myself to him, and perhaps he would allow me a tin of condensed milk, or some other treat!

'On one occasion I had a long talk with a really thoughtful official who commented, "We Communists have great respect for Jesus as a social reformer, but He made the mistake of thinking that society could be changed by love, but we know it can only be changed by hatred" – a true summary of Communist ideas, but a sad one for those who have to live under such an ideology. Such talks were usually on a fairly friendly basis, as they deplored my lack of insight into their good intentions, whilst I was sorry for the way they were going about it, with great plans for "the welfare of the masses" whilst the individuals rotted in misery.'

Local visitors to the foreign doctor under house arrest were very few, for even when there was no sentry on the street door anyone seen entering would be suspect. But on Christmas Day, quite early, there was a tap on his door, and a Chinese woman whom he knew to be a Christian slipped in with a smile and a greeting, to be followed at short intervals by eight or nine other church members. He had been praying that the Lord would give him a special present on this day, and had wondered if it would be an exit visa. This was even better!

'It was a tremendous encouragement to me to know of their continued love and care for me, despite all the poisonous propaganda against foreigners in general, and against me in particular. I asked them if it was not very risky for them to come to see me, but they said it was such a cold morning all the Communists were sitting round their stoves, so it was reasonably safe. We had a lovely time of fellowship. We dared not sing aloud, but had a time of Bible reading and prayer. I remember talking to them from the end of Deuteronomy, where Moses left the Israelites, and Joshua was appointed by the Lord to take over the job.'

His visitors, in the course of their quiet conversation, gave him a little news of what was happening in the outside world. One item, which certainly would not have been considered of

international interest, was extremely hearten-
ing to Rupert, although it in no way affected his
circumstances. It had to do with Tibetans.

'You know there were a few secret Tibetan
believers in Labrang?' one of his visitors said.
'Well, they are meeting quite openly for worship
and prayer now. The Communists have closed
all the lamaseries and set the lamas to work, so
no-one is afraid of them any more.' He thought of
Mr and Mrs Griebenow, and their years of apparently fruitless labour among these people – it had
not been in vain, after all. And the shattering
blows of Communism had not been without a
liberating effect on the lamaistic system, and
the Tibetan people for whom he had a special
concern. It was encouraging.

Meanwhile, his food supplies were running
low, and he was out of cash. He thought of
raiding the hospital stores, where he knew there
was plenty of rice; as it had been bought with
CIM money he would have had no compunction
about using it. However, he knew that if he were
found out by the Communists they would blazon
the matter abroad.

'Mission doctor steals hospital food!' He could
imagine the headlines in newspapers all over
north-west China, and how they would bring
disrepute, not only on him, but on all that he
stood for. So that idea was out.

'So I hung on to the promise which Jesus made
to His followers, "Do not be anxious, saying what
shall we eat, and what shall we drink . . . ? Your
Heavenly Father knows that you have need of
such things. But seek first the Kingdom of God

and His righteousness, and all these thing shall be yours as well." And so when I was down to one very small meal remaining, I waited to see how He would keep that promise, when I was thousands of miles from any obvious source of supply.

'Early that morning the small son of one of the Christian farmers slipped in and asked, "Dr Clarke, how are you off for food?" When I told him I had enough for one small meal, he replied, "Don't worry. My dad will bring you some food this afternoon." Shortly after he had gone the boy of another farmer came in and asked exactly the same question. Never previously had they enquired about this, but when it was necessary the Lord put it into their hearts to do so. Later in the day the two farmers came along with food and said, "Don't worry, whatever the Communists do to you, we won't let you starve." And so far as they were able they kept the promise.'

No sentries were on the door at that time, for the Communists had started meetings for 'self-criticism', in which they had to admit their own errors, and also the errors of others – the more errors of others they could tell, the more they were to be commended, and got off lightly themselves. These meetings stretched on for about six weeks, and by the time they were over the Commissar was the only one who remained in his job.

'Once the meetings were over sentries were again set at my door. So my food supplies were cut off, and soon finished. Once again I remembered the promise of Jesus about food supplies,

but the answer this time seemed to be "No".
The verse from Proverbs came strongly to me,
"Trust in the Lord with all your heart, and lean
not to your own understanding." And I decided
I would stick to the promise in Romans 8 verse
28, that all things work together for good to those
who love God, who have been called according to
His purpose. If my God wanted to test through
starvation, then that was God's business, not
mine. So I lived on a soup of salt and rotting
cabbage leaves for three days, on which diet I
had to take to my bed.'

And that was where he was when the sentry
found him. He was lying on his stomach, as
in that position the discomfort was not quite
so acute. He had given up trying to pray, or
quote Scriptures to encourage himself. All he
could do was to lie on his bed and remember
the well-known verse 'Have faith in God.' But
he had read it two or three days before in a
different translation – Rotherham's – and it
had impressed him then. 'Hold the faithfulness
of God.' Not his faith – but God's faithfulness.

The faithfulness of God. It was over to God now
– His faithfulness. Rupert had come to the end of
any effort himself. The appearance of the sentry
into his room, although it was not immediately
evident, marked the turning point in his affairs.

'What are you doing, lying there in bed in the
daytime? Why haven't you been walking round
the courtyard, exercising yourself?' his captor
demanded abruptly.

Rupert struggled into a sitting position, as
being more respectful, and said,

'Well, you see, I haven't had anything to eat for some time, and I'm quite weak. Light-headed, too, Likely to fall over. So its safer to stay in bed.'

It was a reasonable explanation, as was the answer to the sentry's next question, enquiring *why* he hadn't had anything to eat. 'My food has all gone, and there is no-one to bring me any ...'

The sentry realised that something must be done, and done quickly. It could be very awkward if the prisoner was found dead of starvation. But he had no authority to do the obvious thing, and give him something to eat.

'Write a letter to the Commissar, and I'll see that he gets it,' said the sentry, and provided Rupert with paper and ink to do it.

'My Chinese writing was never very good, but the Commissar got the general idea and when the sentry returned from his evening meal he assured me that the matter would be dealt with on the morrow. Then he dived inside his uniform and produced six steamed breads, saying that he did not want me to go hungry, but not to tell anybody that he had given me police bread. A good local lad – may the Lord bless him!

'On the morrow an official came and made arrangements for my food, and later I was summoned to the Commissar who, in the course of a somewhat lengthy catalogue of my supposed misdoings, accused me of misuse of the hospital medicine, to which I replied in the Chinese version of "Verily, verily, I say unto you, these things are not true." The Commissar took up the words,

and said, "Verily, verily, I say you are a great
liar!" Whereupon we both roared with laughter
– a very unusual occurrence for a Communist
official. I was considerably heartened by his
comparatively friendly manner. And ten days
later I was transferred to Sining. The evident
starvation proved to be one of the "all things"
that God made to turn out for my good, and
another was that as I was too weak to walk, it
was I who rode the mule, and the police escort
who had to do the walking.'

And so he arrived in Sining.

* * *

If Clarence Preedy, standing in the front courtyard of the CIM compound was amazed to see
that the emaciated man weakly dismounting
from a mule was Rupert Clarke, Rupert was
almost equally amazed to find that, after all,
he was not the only CIM missionary left in
China. They looked at each other for a moment
with incredulity, then their faces broadened with
delighted smiles as Clarence hurried forward
exclaiming,

'Rupert! I'd no idea you were coming! How are
you? Here, let me help you . . .'

'Looks like Pharoah's second batch of kine',
was the way he described his appearance when
writing of Rupert's arrival later on. But there
was too much to do for any writing that day.
The only entry in Clarence's diary was:

'April 10. Rupert arrived.'

Once a short but concise cable had been sent

to HQ, 'Inform Jeannette. Arrived Sining. Mailless seven months. Lovingly, Rupert' the most important thing was to give him a good meal and get him to bed. There would be time to bring him up to date with the news after he'd had a good sleep.

In the following days Rupert, thankful for companionship at last, and to have moderately good and satisfying meals, gradually assimilated the information as Clarence imparted it.

'Only eight of us left in China now – four Germans, the Witts and the Hollenwegers in Hunan, and Arthur and Wilda Matthews with little Lilah, and you and I.

'There's plenty of money in the Mission's account. They got three years' rent in advance for that huge property in Shanghai – a miracle, really. The money's all got to be used in China, none of it can be taken out, so there has been no difficulty about paying fines, severance pay, travelling expenses, and so on – when it isn't frozen!

'Jeannette had to face a charge when she got to Lanchow – did you hear about that? Someone she'd dismissed for misconduct from the hospital there, years ago, took advantage of the opportunity to get her own back. Jeannette got let off with a fine, which the Mission paid of course, so it wasn't too bad, though a bit tense at the time.

'The Matthews have been having a pretty grim time of it. They walked into trouble as soon as they arrived in Hwangyuen. Instead of having the Mission house they weren't allowed in it – just had a kitchen, and a bedroom on the

other side of the courtyard and up a flight of
stairs. Unheated, of course. Imagine Wilda carrying that baby girl across the courtyard in the
snow, and leaving her in that icy room. They've
given it up, of course – they just live and sleep
in the kitchen.

'Arthur had to face an accusation meeting,
brought by a woman in Changyeh, where he
was earlier. He signed a confession admitting
all five counts. It had us howling with laughter
when we read it. He was accused of:

'Standing on a table belonging to the church.
(It was rickety, and the church didn't want it.)

'Misusing a memorial plaque.

'Locking the kitchen door of the church.

'Closing the school at Changyeh. (These in
accordance with the church and school's wishes.)

'Killing a dog. (The dog was a stray, and the
deacon asked him to kill it.)

'The matter was finally solved by payment of
US $135 to the lady who had been offended.

'But the Matthews are having their financial
difficulties too, like me. Worse, in a way – Arthur
has to go and plead for their allowance every
time, and then he's kept waiting around outside
the office for hours on end, like a beggar.'

Not that Clarence did not have his difficulties when it came to drawing his money each
month from the Mission account in the Government Bank. If the rig'·t government official was
contacted Clarence could draw the money, but
sometimes he was not available – or did not feel
inclined to sign the necessary permission for the
money to be withdrawn. On one such occasion

Clarence and Rupert, nearly at the end of their resources, prayed together about the verses 'Do not be anxious . . . your Heavenly Father knows that you have need of all these things.' Then they went for their daily walk, round and round the courtyard, and as they did so Rupert noticed a bundle of paper on the ground. Picking it up, he discovered it was a roll of bank notes!

'We never discovered whence they came, but probably they had fallen from the pocket of one of the black-uniformed police that patrolled our flat roofs. Anyway, we rapidly converted them into food, and reckoned that, like Elijah's, it had been brought by the ravens.

'Just before Christmas we were again getting low on food. We had potatoes and beans left, but felt that that was a poor way to celebrate Christmas. So we humbly asked the true Father of Christmas to provide a little luxury for the occasion. On Christmas Eve a Chinese man came in, explaining that as he passed our door he remembered that he owed Clarence a little money for something he had purchased a year or two before. God caused him to remember and repay just at the right time to enable us to have some comparative luxury for Christmas.'

Soon after Christmas their agents in Shanghai learned that it was reasonably safe to send barknotes through the post, so from that time they were no longer dependent for their cash on the availability and amiability of the official at the Government Bank. They were thankful for that, and thankful, too, for each other's company. It made housekeeping more interesting and the uncertainty of their situation easier to bear. And as they read the Bible, alone and then together, it kept hope alive and nourished patience to share their thoughts, providing a never-failing escape from the monotony of life in the confinement of the compound.

So it continued until early March, when suddenly, late one morning, the gate of the compound was opened and instead of an official and a couple of policemen, a coolie appeared carrying some shabby looking luggage, followed by a woman leading a child by the hand. She was dressed in a Chinese gown, but they recognised her immediately. It was Wilda Matthews and Lilah. Then the gate closed – there was no sign of Arthur. He had not been allowed to leave.

'I was hoping that we could all leave together, but one morning, after I'd been pleading with the Lord that it might be so, I was confronted with Romans 9 verse 21,' Wilda told them. ' "Hath not the potter power over the clay?" So I faced it squarely. All I could do was to bow my head and say "Not my will, but Thine be done." It's a comfort to be able to leave it all with the Lord.

'Yes, I've got my exit visa and travel permit,' she continued, relating what had happened in Hwangyuan. 'They said they were letting me go because I've got no more money, but they'd keep Arthur behind because they had serious charges against him – against Dr Clarke, too. The regime knows how to deal with criminals, they said!'

It was easy enough to guess what charge would be brought against Rupert. Murder! There would be no difficulty in bringing a case against a doctor, for what doctor has never had patients wh ، have eventually died? No-one knew what the Communists were holding against Arthur, but they had evidently finished with Clarence. He was allowed to escort Wilda Matthews and her little girl out of China.

'That left me on my own in Sining, and Arthur alone in Hwangyuan, the last of the CIM in China. What happened about my food supply after that I do not remember. I am sure I did not go to see the surly official, and I don't remember being allowed out to buy food – that part of my time under house arrest remains very hazy ... until 5 July. It was the fifth anniversary of the opening of the Holy Light Clinic, and the second of my release from the Hwalung gaol, so I asked the Lord for a very special celebration of the date. Nothing happened obviously that day – but the official wheels began to turn, as later in the month I had a visit from the police. They told me to pack up my things (half a kit-bag of them) and come with them to the provincial gaol. This proved to be a great improvement on the one in Hwalung. I had a cell to myself, and was fed with some quite nice Chinese food.'

And what was even better – that very evening he got a glimpse of the prisoner in a cell opposite. It was Arthur Matthews! The tide was beginning to turn!

The following day Rupert was escorted to a public meeting of about a thousand people. He found himself with two other prisoners – both

Germans, Roman Catholic priests, one of whom
was a Bishop.

'A whole lot of the oddest charges were read out
against us. One was that the Bishop professed
to be a religious leader, but he was actually the
possessor of a complete set of carpenter's tools. It
might have been thought to be a recommendation
in a "Worker's Republic", but it was solemnly
read out against him, and also that he had run
an orphanage ... Then it was announced that
we had confessed to all the odd crimes that were
charged against us, many of which we had never
even heard of. Then the judge got up to read the
sentence to be passed upon us.

'We were immediately, and eternally, to be
expelled from China!'

The three prisoners had learned by this time
to hide their feelings. The relief that swelled
up within them had to be suppressed, and they
managed to look dismayed and downcast, as
reporters swarmed around and cameras clicked.
To Rupert's relief, he saw Arthur being brought
across the courtyard to join them. He had been
locked in another room, with the threat of a
separate public trial being held for him, but the
policeman escorting him read out the charges
against him, folded the paper, still unsigned,
and shouted,

'Everlasting deportation! To be put into immediate effect!'

They spent the night in an inn, well guarded,
and the following day a policeman came and told
them to get ready to leave, the train would be
going in about an hour. Six armed guards with

revolvers hustled them to the station and onto the train, and they were off.

On the whole, it was quite a pleasant journey, not unlike a Cook's tour, Rupert observed later. Compartments were emptied on the crowded trains so that the guards, with their prisoners, could travel in some comfort. They were held up for two days in Tienshui, and the four prisoners were put in the gaol there, but were given comfortable cells, and treated so casually that the two Roman Catholic priests, who had endured about eighteen months in a prison in Tsinghai, could scarcely believe they were not in an ordinary inn. But when it came to dinner time, and one of the gaolers enquired, 'What would you like to eat?' they were speechless.

They were being asked what they would like to eat! In prison! They were too surprised to reply.

So was Arthur. He looked at the questioner blankly, thinking he had misunderstood what was said. After two and a half years of confrontations with the Head of Police in Hwangyuan, this could not be real!

Only Rupert kept his head. True to type, he reflected gravely for a minute, then made his decision. He felt he could answer for them all. There had been very few pigs in Tsinghai, where they had come from, it being a Muslim area, so he knew what they would like, what would be a treat for them all.

'What would you like to eat?'

With a polite nod of the head, Rupert gave the order.

'We'd like sweet and sour pork, thank you,' he said.

* * *

It had been a very hot, humid day in the CIM office in Hong Kong, and it was just a few minutes before five o'clock when the telephone rang. Rather wearily, for he was tired, the secretary lifted the receiver, then stiffened suddenly. He could scarcely believe what he was hearing.

'Two of your people have just crossed the border. Dr Rupert Clarke and Mr Arthur Matthews.' It was an old Roman Catholic priest speaking. He had been meeting the trains bringing people out of China every day for years, and knew exactly what to do. 'Their passports had been taken from them, but some temporary papers have been written here, so there is no problem. We'll put them on the next train. Goodbye!' The receiver was replaced, and then a shout rang out down the corridor.

'Praise the Lord! They're out! Clarke and Matthews! Over the border! Coming in on the next train! Clarke and Matthews! They're out! Get ready . . . !'

Fifty minutes later the train from the border drew in at Kowloon station, and eager eyes scanned the passengers, searching for two westerners among the thronging Chinese. There they were! Arthur Matthews smiling rather shyly, Rupert erect and doffing a trilby hat . . .

Sixty-eight years had passed since young Hudson Taylor on the beach at Brighton, conscious of a divine impelling, had founded the China Inland Mission. During that period its members had travelled and settled freely throughout the thickly populated land, encountering danger and hardship certainly, but in the main without official opposition. They had gone, urged on by the realization that beyond them were regions where Christ was not known, that no others had gone before them. They were pioneers.

That period was over. As Rupert and Arthur passed over the bridge to Hong Kong they were unconsciously marking the end of an era. The Mission to Inland China had ceased to exist.

Not that they had any sense of making history. What they were conscious of was that their personal ordeals were over. Behind them now were the long months of confinement, the tension of uncertainty right up to the time when they had started passing along the long low buildings, the barbed wire fences, to the last of the Communist guards. There had been a hold up then, with the ever present threat of a last minute accusation that would prevent them from stepping on to the iron bridge at the other end of which a Union Jack was fluttering. But the harangue which one of the officials had commenced had been peremptorily cut short by another, and they had been hurried on – to freedom. Arthur Matthews and Rupert Clarke – the last of the CIM to leave China.

They were too exhausted, physically and emotionally, to react with great enthusiasm to the welcome they received. As Rupert expressed it,

'It was good to be amongst our own people again, and to have a real bath and get into some clean clothes – but we had been travelling too much for us to feel any great elation – just a quiet thankfulness to the kind Heavenly Father who had brought us out at last.

'In those days there was no direct telephone from Hong Kong to Johannesburg so that I could not carry out my intended plan of calling Jeannette, and had to be content with sending a telegram, which was not nearly so exciting.' But arrangements were made as quickly as possible for him to rejoin her, and two days after arriving in Hong Kong he boarded a BOAC plan for Karachi. There was a delay when it developed engine trouble and had to turn back, emptying its petrol tanks over the sea, much to Rupert's dismay. What a waste! he thought, remembering the difficulty of obtaining fuel for the hospital jeep away on the Tibetan border. But he arrived in Karachi with two days to spare before catching the plan for Nairobi, where he spent another two days in the Africa Inland Mission Rest Home. Then it was on to Johannesburg.

He was the last passenger to emerge from Immigration, having been kept behind because he had truthfully admitted on the form he had to fill in that he had been in prison. When he had the opportunity to explain that it was a prison in Communist China he was allowed to pass through immediately, but by that time the long corridor was deserted, at the end of which a rather anxious little group was waiting. Jeannette had begun to fear he had not arrived, when suddenly Humphrey broke away and started running. A figure had just appeared at the end of the corridor and Humphrey saw that his face was the same as the one he had looked at after saying his prayers at bedtime for the past two years.

'Kiss Daddy goodnight,' Jeannette had said, and Humphrey had kissed the photo. Now Daddy was here! As Rupert wrote to friends a few days later,

'The little boy cannot possibly have remembered me, for he was only eighteen months when he left, but he just made one flying leap into my arms, and has been telling all and sundry ever since how nice it is to have a "real Daddy"!'

8

A new posting

Recovery from the tensions and privations of the past two years did not take place immediately. It was evident that Rupert was undernourished physically and he needed relaxation to begin the slow process of realizing that he was free. But he started dealing almost at once with the pile of correspondence that had mounted up. Writing a long letter dated 30 July 1953, to be duplicated and sent to the many friends who had written, he commenced with the words.

'Up until 8th of this month life was going on just about as dully as usual, except that I had received hardly any mail for three weeks, and was wondering what it was all about; when there was a rap at the door and three people from the police department escorted by the Chinese pastor arrived, and told me to get packed up and to come with them straightaway to the police station. Naturally I reckoned that I was in for another spell in prison, but . . .' followed by a very full description of his deportation from China with Arthur Matthews, and eventual arrival in South Africa.

'People have been very kind to us, and given me a most kindly welcome, whilst the Press has only just discovered that I have arrived, so that all has been peaceful and quiet.' Apart from a short talk in church, only one central meeting had been arranged, which, as he observed, was rather ambiguously advertised 'Dr Clarke will tell of his adventures in the YWCA'. This was followed by a seaside holiday in Natal before moving back to England.

'By this time I was much better physically, but recognised that I was poorly off technically, so began to look round for a suitable post graduate course to bring me up to date again. The first appointment was as a locum in general practice near Cambridge, which was a very happy time, and at the end of the month the Christian GP offered me a partnership in the firm. He told me I had done my bit, and could now retire from the mission field.'

The offer was an attractive one, not one to be lightly refused, so he and Jeannette talked it over. The door to China was closed permanently for them, that was evident, and Chinese was the only Asian language he and Jeannette had mastered. To start learning a new language, and become integrated into a new culture in middle life would be no easy undertaking.

Furthermore, their missionary society, the China Inland Mission, had already entered an entirely new phase in its existence. In China it had been a pioneer mission, establishing its centres of work where no other messenger of Christ crucified had been. Those days were over.

No longer could the mission describe itself as being to inland China – in fact, the very name China carried with it overtones of communism. The name was changed to Overseas Missionary Fellowship. In the countries in south and east Asia to which its members were now going, other missions had been working for decades. However, in those countries there were not only sizeable Chinese minorities, but many areas where no missionaries were living, providing openings for pioneer evangelism, even though there were already indigenous churches in these countries. But in such circumstances, the whole approach to missionary activity must be different. The OMF moved with wise caution, and for medical men in particular there seemed very little likelihood of immediate openings, and Rupert was essentially a doctor, not an evangelist. Was it wise to turn down this opening with its opportunity for the use of his skills in his own country?

And there was Humphrey to consider now. What would it mean to him, an only child, to be separated from both his parents if they went to live and work in some remote area in a country in the Far East? The thought of leaving him, a lonely little boy put into a boarding school, was heart-rending, and made the security of a settled home and medical practice all the more inviting. They talked it over and decided to pray about it before giving an answer to the very kind and generous doctor who had made the offer.

Guidance came imperceptibly, but for both of them it was quite clear. It came through the words spoken by Jesus to the erstwhile disciple who wanted his family affairs settled first.

'No man, having put his hand to the plough, and looking back, is fit for the kingdom of God.'

There was no question as to what plough they had put their hands. They knew that for them the commission to go into all the world and make disciples of all nations had never been rescinded. For Rupert, with his military background, the time in England could be regarded rather as waiting for a new posting. So they agreed that the kind offer was not in God's plan for them, and Rupert started looking around for a registrarship in general surgery. After several unsuccessful applications he was put in touch, through the Christian Medical Fellowship, with the ortheopaedic surgeon of the Royal Surrey County Hospital in Guildford, who was looking for a registrar for the orthopaedic and accident department.

'He wondered if I was fit enough to do the job, but I assured him that we had just been hiking across the Pennine Way, which was encouraging to him! Orthopaedics had always struck me as rather a dull subject, but for want of a better offer I accepted the job and thoroughly enjoyed two years of mainly accident surgery. The women's ward was almost entirely filled with old ladies who had fallen and "broken their hips", whilst the men's ward was largely filled with young men who had survived motor-cycle crashes, but we managed to fit in a certain amount of genuine orthopaedic surgery also.'

Family-wise it was a particularly congenial

period, for they occupied a flat in the beautiful Regency house of General Sir Arthur Smith, set in its own grounds, not far from Guildford. Schooling for Humphrey presented no problem, but finding a suitable church was different. For the first two or three Sundays they went to the parish church in the village, but the only part of the service that he enjoyed was when the collection plate came round and he dropped his coin into it from as high as he could reach, so that it landed with a plop. For the rest, he asserted that it was boring.

'As we privately quite agreed with him, we transferred to the Guildford Baptist Church, which all of us enjoyed. Humphrey liked to sit with us in the gallery, and it became quite a looked-forward-to ritual each Sunday, when the youngsters left for the "Children's Church" for Humphrey to descend and march up the aisle last of them all, to bestow a beaming smile upon the minister before disappearing to the back regions of the church.'

It was during this period that what appeared to be a simple little incident occurred that was to have a significant bearing on the future lives of all three of them. It happened when they were in Scotland on holiday, visiting some of Jeannette's relations. She and Humphrey were out together for a walk, and had come to a low wall on which they sat for a short time, admiring the scenery, when Humphrey voiced a question that had been perplexing him.

'Mummy,' he said, 'How do people become Christians? What do you have to do?'

Jeannette looked down on her little son, and gave him a simple answer. He knew about the Lord Jesus, His death on the cross, His resurrection, His ascension into Heaven – it was unnecessary to explain it all to him. The child had heard it many times already, and believed it without question.

What do I have to do to become a Christian? he wanted to know, and his mother told him. The Lord Jesus was standing at the door of his heart, knocking. All Humphrey had to do was to open the door and ask Jesus to come in. Did he want to do that?

Yes, he did. So sitting on the wall, they sang together, quietly, the words of the chorus,

> Into my heart
> Into my heart
> Come into my heart, Lord Jesus.
> Come in today
> Come in to stay,
> Come into my heart, Lord Jesus.

Just as simply had Rupert, as a young medical student, done the same thing. 'I knelt by my bed, and took the twentieth verse of Revelation chapter 3. "Behold, I stand at the door, and knock; if any man hear My voice and open the door, I will come in to him, and will sup with him, and he with Me." And I just asked the Lord Jesus to come into my heart and to stay with me. At the time I felt no difference at all, but I never had any doubt that Christ was in me, and I in Him . . .'

So it was with Humphrey. He sat on the wall

for a minute or two without saying anything, then slithered down to the ground and continued the walk with his mother in quite a natural way, just like any other small boy. But from that time he knew he was a Christian, and when the test came he was ready for it.

Meanwhile, Rupert's two years' registrarship came to an end, and the Overseas Missionary Fellowship was feeling its way in the changing international scene in the East. The days of colonialism were coming to an end. The French were being forced out of Indo-China, the British were withdrawing from Malaya, the Americans were encouraging independence in the Philippine Islands, and the Dutch were overthrown in the East Indies. Throughout the colonial period the little country of Siam (Thailand) had retained its sovereignty, and it was here, in its central provinces, that the Overseas Missionary Fellowship was establishing its first hospital. Built in the paddy-fields near Manorom, the doctors Chris and Catherine Maddox were already installed, and others were ready to join them. In Rupert's view it was adequately supplied with doctors without him. Remembering the shortage of staff at Hwalung he may have wondered what he would find to do at Manorom!

He and Jeannette continued to pray for some other opening, and after long waiting the answer came suddenly and unmistakeably, pointing to what was to be his new posting.

* * *

During the hundred and more years of Dutch
domination in Indonesia Christian missionaries
from Holland had established Protestant churches
which had somehow survived the violent period
of post-war revolution, and now that things were
settling down there were openings for evangelism
and Bible teaching which members of OMF were
slowly entering. Rupert and Jeannette, always
loyal to the mission in which they had served,
followed the progress of the work in their steady
way, praying each day for the topics outlined in
the prayer calendar. As they did so, they found
their thoughts turning more and more towards
Indonesia, although the OMF had no medical
work there.

'Then one day we received a letter from our old
friend, David Bentley-Taylor, who had recently
settled in the village of Turen, near Malang in
East Java. His house was opposite a Salvation
Army hospital, which had had no doctor for the
eight years since its return from military occupation. But the Canadian Salvation Army Captain
in charge wondered if perhaps OMF would lend
a doctor to help them out . . .'

Little wonder that as they read these words
Rupert and Jeannette saw them to be the answer
to their prayers. OMF leaders readily agreed to
Rupert's filling the vacancy, and so applications for visas were duly made. Then came a
hold-up to which missionary societies were to
become increasingly familiar in the years that
lay ahead. Visas for Dr and Mrs Rupert Clarke to
enter Indonesia were withheld. Nearly two years
passed before they were eventually granted –

two years in which Rupert spent most of his time doing short-term temporary jobs in hospitals, gaining experience which proved extremely helpful later on. Then, early in 1958, although visas had not yet been granted, 'we moved to Singapore for a crash course in Malay language, a tongue closely akin to Indonesian.

'Singapore, even in those days, was a lovely place, with a refreshing blend of East and West, and thither the headquarters of the OMF had moved. It was good to spend some time there, right opposite the Botanic Gardens, before moving to a small house on the edge of a Malay *kampong* (village) for concentrated language study. Later we moved to a large, colonial style house on the sea shore at Pasir Panjang, about five miles west of Singapore city, to continue our language study on our own. Swarms of golden orioles and bulbuls in the palm trees in the garden proved rather distracting! In May I had the opportunity to go to Manorom to visit the "Paddy Field Hospital" – a five-day hot train journey through dusty stubble fields from which the rice had recently been harvested. The visit to Manorom was a good refresher as to the running of a mission hospital, and included a Landrover trip up to Chiengmai to deliver some leprosy patients to the settlement there, as Manorom did not yet have the facilities to give them prolonged care.'

Rupert's journey back to Singapore from Bangkok was by ship, on one of the very old China coast ships he had watched coming into Chefoo harbour twenty years previously, and when he arrived back it was to learn that visas for Indonesia would eventually be forthcoming. They were actually issued in July, and as Humphrey was already happily installed in the school for missionaries' children in Malaysia there was nothing to hinder them proceeding at once.

'So we made haste to get going and arrived in Jakarta, the capital of Indonesia, on 5 August. There we were met by Salvation Army officers and made welcome at their Officers' Training Home. We had a quick train trip up to their headquarters in Bandung, then on to Surabaya to register at the Department of Immigration and up to Turen, 1,000 ft above the steamy shore.'

How different it all was from the barren, bleak Tibetan border! Here were swarms of birds, especially of the finch tribe, making it an ornithologist's paradise; rice fields giving a yield of five crops every two years; a good irrigation system supplying extract of volcanic ash from Mount Smeru which provided almost all the fertilizer that was needed. Luxuriant vegetation. And from Rupert's point of view, a splendidly built hospital, a one storey complex of eighty-five beds. But it had its drawbacks.

'It had been very comprehensively stripped by the various armies which had occupied it during the war and revolution, and very few surgical instruments remained. And so one of our first moves was for Captain Kjelson to drive us back to Surabaya to procure a basic surgical kit in the surgical instruments shops there. There was quite a nicely built operating set up, but unfortunately it had been designed in the northern hemisphere and faced north, attracting all the tropical sunlight. The electricity supply was very poor, and it was some years before we could procure a reliable generator to power an air-conditioned unit in the operating theatre. The hospital had been run by nurses as a sort of medical nursing home, with only an occasional visit from a government doctor, so that any idea of surgery was viewed by the locals with considerable suspicion.

'But then the mother-in-law of a local policeman slashed her throat! I was summoned with great urgency to the poor woman, who was blue in the face as blood bubbled in and out of her airway. The insertion of a tracheostomy tube made a vast improvement, and then we took her to the government hospital in Malang eighteen miles north, where she made a good recovery – and so the policeman was saved from the appalling loss of face of a mother-in-law's suicide.

'After that we had officialdom on our side, and we thanked God for their encouragement to bring all surgical problems to us – mostly road accidents and knife wounds. Jeannette was in control of the operating theatre, and had to train her aides to use large kerosene pressure stoves to sterilize the cloths in oversize rice steamers, to boil up instruments in pans, and to boil vast kettles of water for the washing of hands, swabs, and so on. These aides were mostly girls from the Christian villages of the south coast of Java, and had primary education only, but some of them showed excellent ability in the theatre, and were thoroughly reliable, cheerful and resilient. They needed to be, when operating sessions were often twelve hours long!

'The operating lists on Tuesdays and Fridays tended to start at the top end of the body with eye surgery, cataracts and so on; then progress down to the neck to deal with thyroid lumps and bumps which were very common; thence to the abdomen, usually for the removal of bladder stones; and so on to the legs where amputation was frequently needed for gangrene caused by cigarette smoking. Toddlers were encouraged to smoke upon their mothers' knees, and it was not surprising that arterial blockage from "Buergers disease" brought on gangrene, even among teenagers.

'Frequent night emergencies were mostly for Caesarian sections for obstructed childbirth, and it was very pleasing to see that, by a policy of encouragement of the old village midwives, these unfortunates were brought to us earlier and earlier, with great improvement in survival. Otherwise, apart from the occasional obstructed hernia, most loss of sleep was for ex-sanguinated women who had had "back-street abortions." We did our best to encourage modern birth control methods instead, but many of them implored us to remove the womb, and we found that, with no blood available for transfusions, a simple hysterectomy proved the safest method.'

It is doubtful whether Rupert ever worked harder at any time in his life than during that first term of service in Java. He was the only doctor in the hospital, and as his reputation increased, so did his work load. Operating sessions lasting eight hours might be followed by night calls to patients living miles away, and the overall medical responsibility he had to shoulder alone. He probably managed to maintain his health and strength by observing the divine law of keeping one day in seven as a day of rest, and this he did in a very practical manner.

'Wednesday was our day off. After a swift round of the wards, we would go off on our bicycles to explore the countryside, or go by hospital car to one of the nearby hill resorts which had swimming pools. Once a month the girls who worked in the theatre came with us in the car to one of the resorts, or to one of the Christian villages on the south coast, where the bathing was good – provided one avoided sea urchins and other painful creatures.'

There were times when Rupert got discouraged by the pressure of work, day and night, and the comparatively slender spiritual results that he saw. One day, in an unusual burst of self revelation, he voiced his feelings. He was speaking to Alex Pronoto, a pastor who was widely known and respected throughout Java, and a close friend of David Bentley-Taylor's. The Gospel was proclaimed one way and another in the hospital, Christian literature was made available, and yet very, very rarely did a patient come to faith in Jesus Christ, Rupert complained. The response he received was so prompt and definite that it surprised him.

'Don't you give up!' said Pastor Pronoto urgently. 'Even if you personally never see a single soul turn to Christ, don't you give up! I go out to the Muslim villages, and as a Christian evangelist

I'm not very welcome. But when I say that I'm connected with the hospital in Turen, every door is open to me!' And in a land where open air preaching was forbidden, the entrance into homes was essential.

If spiritual results in the hospital itself seemed meagre, there was one area that was particularly fruitful, and that was among the nurse aides. On Sundays Jeannette held a Bible class for the staff, and most of the nurses attended. They came from the 'Christian' villages, but in most cases their faith was nominal, and as Rupert wrote,

'It was very encouraging to see a number of these girls come to know and love the Lord Jesus for themselves.' And they became ardent young evangelists. 'On the evenings of operating days they went round the wards reading a little Scripture, singing hymns and praying for the patients.

'One of these patients was from quite a fanatic Islamic home. As he heard the cheerful singing, of which there is none in Islam, heard the aides asking the Heavenly Father to heal his typhoid fever (while every Muslim knows that Allah is far too distant and too busy to worry about individuals, and none would dare to call him Father) he determined to find out more about the Jesus way. He returned to us as an enthusiastic Christian chauffeur/handy-man, and married one of the nurse aides. Then he left us to become chauffeur to a local pastor who owned a jeep, but when that worthy crashed the jeep he had to turn to taxi driving. But his most prosperous days were Sundays, and he attended church less

and less, to the distress of his wife.' So subtly does
the pull of the world exercise its power over the
unwary! 'But his wife prayed that the Lord would
get him back into Christian employment, and her
prayers were answered when a whole bunch of
taxi drivers were summoned to the police traffic
department and warned that as they already
had two endorsements on their licences (chiefly
for overloading their taxi minibuses) they only
needed one more endorsement to lose their public
service driving licences, as well as go to prison.
They were not greatly worried about a spell in
gaol, but the threat of losing his licence persuaded this driver to return to the hospital's
employment, to the great joy of his wife. He
remained with us for some years, and was a
real 'pillar' of the hospital, eventually leaving
to become a Salvation Army officer.'

* * *

In 1963 the Clarkes returned to England on
furlough, and were motoring in Scotland with
Humphrey when Rupert developed abdominal
pain and ended up in Dumfries as a patient
in the hospital there. 'They had a look inside,
and decided to treat with antibiotics for about
a month. At the same time Humphrey developed appendicitis, so we were both in the same
hospital. After a month or so we all headed
south again. But I was very cold and shivery at
nights, and was glad to spend most of that hard
winter of 1963 in the pleasantly warm wards of
the Middlesex hospital, as it took a long time

to control those malarial rigors. An operation revealed a rather obscure gut inflammation, but the affected area was successfully removed, so that we were able to plan for a return to Java.' So ended a furlough largely dominated by physical disorders for Rupert, and in order to provide a sort of convalescent cruise, it was arranged that they should return to Java by boat.

During the cruise the chief engineer began to suffer with excrutiating toothache – and there was no dentist aboard. Rupert quietly offered to do what he could, and finding a set of dental forceps and some local anaesthetics, painlessly extracted the offending molar. Out of gratitude for this service the Blue Funnel captain kept the Clarke's baggage in a locked cabin when they arrived in Jakarta, preserving it from plundering hands at the port, and then held it safely suspended in a cargo-net until they were ready to take delivery.

It was as well that he did so, for they had returned to a country where the economy was going downhill very rapidly. Government officials were paid a pittance, and made up the rest by corruption and theft. Roads were unmended, buildings dilapidated, motor transport mostly immobilised for lack of spare parts, and train time-tables were completely unreliable. The country was ripe for revolution, and Communists were increasingly active. It was rumoured that the names of Christian missionaries, along with the leaders of other religions, were high on the list for 'liquidation'. However, although the Communist's attempted coup in October was promptly overthrown, there

followed a period of terrible carnage. All who were
suspected of having Communist sympathies were
'outlawed, with the result that militant Muslims
could attack homes and villages, killing, raping,
plundering, and the victims had no legal protection from the authorities. It was a harrowing time
for those in the hospital in Turen. Although they
knew nothing of the attempted coup until it was
over, they saw the terrible results of revenge by
fanatic Islam. In some of the nearby villages not
one adult male survived. For months the roads
were too dangerous for people to call Rupert out
to see a patient at night, and although he deplored
the reason for this, it had one good outcome as far
as he was concerned. After the usual heavy day
in the hospital, he could be sure, at last, of a good
night's rest. When at last things settled down,
and President Sukarno was ousted by General
Suharto whose wiser policies gained the support
of western governments and the economy began
to improve, people had got out of the habit of
calling out the doctor at night – 'a real boon
for us, and rarely a disaster for the patients,'
observed Rupert, and then went on to record
something of great significance for the Christian
Church in Java.

Some years before the attempted coup Alex
Pronoto, whose denominational background was
Presbyterian, had come to the conclusion that
infant baptism had become a superstition, and
decided to stop the practice. He would only bap-
tise on confession of faith by the person involved.
So that stopped infant baptism.

'But one day the child of a recently baptised

couple toddled in front of a motor car and was killed,' wrote Rupert. The Islamic authorities removed the body and buried it according to Islamic custom, as the child was still officially of Islam. 'Needless to say, that did the child no harm, but was very distressing to the parents. A few months' later a child of Christian parents died in our hospital from cerebral malaria, but the same performance was repeated.'

That the children of Christian parents should be given a Muslim burial disturbed the whole Christian community, and it was then that Pronoto decided that if the parents believed, the whole family should be baptised. 'I know that doesn't mean they are "born again", but legally they become Christian, and it is my responsibility to lead them into Christ's kingdom,' he said. After the attempted coup his decision proved to be a very wise one – surely guided by God Himself, who alone knows what the future holds. Reacting strongly against atheistic Communism, the Government ruled that everyone must have a religion, and that religious instruction was to be given in all schools. Those who did not have a certificate of Christian baptism, therefore, were compelled to attend Islamic classes, whilst those who were officially Christian were given Bible teaching. The outcome of this ruling was that, in actual fact, the syllabus for Christian teaching in all Government schools was drawn up and written by Leatha Humes of the OMF and her team in Jakarta.

Meanwhile work in the hospital continued as busy as ever. 'The casualty department was very crowded, with up to two hundred patients some days, so I used to turn over some of the minor surgery to the operating theatre for Jeannette to deal with. One of the patients was a middle-aged woman who needed to have fluid run from her abdomen about every three weeks because of cirrhosis of the liver which is quite frequent in rural Java. The "tapping" had to be done rather slowly, so as to avoid undue shock, and as it went on Jeannette used to try to explain to her the way of salvation through Jesus. But Jeannette's Indonesian was not perfect, and the patient was a rustic Javanese, knowing little of the national language, so Jeannette turned to the Muslim aide who was helping her, to ask if she thought that the patient understood what she had been told.

' "I'm not sure whether she really understands – but I do!" was the unexpected reply, "And I'm going to follow Jesus!" And very brightly she did! After she graduated she married a planter from one of the Christian villages.' It was typical of Rupert and Jeannette that when they had the opportunity they made the long journey to the distant coffee estate to find out how she was progressing in her new found faith, and came back completely satisfied. She was going on very well with the Lord, Rupert reported.

In the busy life of the hospital, however, such experiences were rare. Increasingly large numbers of people were coming to see the doctor, and Rupert found it impossible to deal with them all. He did not hesitate to delegate authority where he recognised ability, and one of the missionary nurses, Margaret Young, was left to attend to the many patients who came along with malaria, and vitamin B deficiencies. In obedience to his instructions, most of the malarial cases were treated with an initial transmuscular injection of quinine and Urethana – 'and despite the horror stories of the text books, I only once saw an abscess from our injections,' he reported, adding quickly, 'and that was a child I myself had injected when on a home visit.'

Not only was he the doctor in the hospital, but he had to turn dentist as well to alleviate the suffering of those who came along with raging toothache. These dental extractions he dealt with on what he called 'the conveyor belt system.' The patients were all lined up, seated on benches, and given anaesthetic injections in rotation. By the time the last one had received the injection the first was ready for the extraction. But he had taken the precaution, unobtrusively, to ensure that the first patient was a phlegmatic type of person, and that the extraction would be an easy one. 'I found it had a good psychological effect on the others.'

Dental extractions came into the category of minor operations, and so were dealt with later in the day. However, exceptions were made for those who had come a long distance. They were his patients, and he was not indifferent to their circumstances. So he saw to it that their teeth were pulled out in time for them to catch the last bus home.

It was this sort of care that helped to enhance the reputation of the doctor in Turen.

9

Doctor in Java

When David Ellis, as a young worker, was appointed to Indonesia, he listened respectfully when that seasoned missionary, Dr Rupert Clarke, his senior in years as well as in experience, offered him a word of advice. Perhaps to his surprise, it had nothing to do with prayer, or preaching, or adapting to local culture, or anything like that. It was very down to earth.

'Young man,' said Rupert. 'Don't forget to take your day off each week,' then he added, 'And get out – and *walk!*' Ellis nodded meekly, and soon discovered that the doctor always was down to earth. When young workers at a conference started talking of what they termed spiritual depression, the doctor added very little to the discussions.

'Spiritual depression is 99% in the blood,' he asserted, adding that it was best dealt with by healthy sleeping and eating habits, and proper exercise. Nor was he any more forthcoming in replying to the missionary who had worked out an elaborate schedule for taking various vitamins etc., daily, thinking it ought to be adopted by others. It was sent to him first, to ask for his assessment. His reply was quite courteous, but brief: 'The vitamins you are taking will do you no harm.' And he had a cavalier attitude towards what he termed bureaucracy. The OMF had business-like methods in finance, and all its workers were called upon to render accounts of money committed to them for their work. When David Ellis was appointed as superintendent in Indonesia, he had the responsibility of collecting them all, and forwarding them to headquarters in Singapore.

'Accounts were not Rupert's strong point, but they were always 100% accurate,' he said with a chuckle. 'No accountant could fault them, I am sure. Here is an example: "Money received ... 125,000 Rupias. Money spent ... 125,000 Rupias." There the account began and ended.'

From time to time questionnaires were sent out regarding living conditions and general expenses. The reason for this was that while all members of the Fellowship, whether in senior or junior positions, received the same quarterly remittance, it was realized that the cost of living varied in different locations and countries. It was more expensive to live in Japan, for instance, than in a tribal village in north Thailand, so remittances must be adapted accordingly. On one occasion, before sending back the completed questionnaires, Ellis glanced at Rupert's, and was surprised to see all the pages were blank, except for a comment on the last one. It was to the effect that he had no time to answer a lot

of questions invented by people sitting in offices
who had nothing else to do but ask questions that
other people were too busy to answer.

'There was nothing you could do about it – you
just had to grin!' said Ellis, relating the incident
years later. Everyone at HQ knew Rupert. They
knew, too, the quality of his medical work, and
his ingenuity in keeping expenses down. But
Ellis, in his capacity as superintendent, knew
him more intimately than most of them, and saw
for himself the effect he had on the people among
whom he lived.

'His name went throughout the whole great
land of Java. In Indonesia doctors are regarded
as people of tremendous importance, right at the
top. You don't expect the doctor to come to you.
You have to go to the doctor – or be carried to him!
But one day, right over in West Java, a man said
to me, "You know that doctor in East Java. He's
different from other people. When people are ill
he actually gets on a bicycle and goes to see them!
I've heard that when people are sick in a village,
he actually gets on a bicycle and goes into the
country! He's a *doctor* – and he does that!"'

On one occasion Ellis himself had the opportunity of observing Rupert's quite unselfconscious
care for his patients. He had to see Rupert
about some important mission business, and
the only way of seeing him was in the hospital
– at work.

'I went down to the hospital, and right into the
operating theatre. There he was, with Jeannette,
they were working on what looked to me like a
sort of bottle. Rupert just said to me as I came

in, "Don't you knock against anything with your unsterilised clothing!" I didn't, and stood there and watched him remove with incredible skill a massive goitre from the patient. We had our discussion over the body of the person in question, but once the operation was over, he didn't just go and wash up, and let somebody else take care of the patient.' This was what Ellis was expecting – and he thought their discussion could then be carried on more normally. Instead, what he saw was Rupert himself putting the patient on the trolley, then he saw the back of him 'two hairy legs sticking out below a pair of little white shorts, and what looked like a butcher's apron flapping . . . he was wheeling the patient back into the ward himself, and seeing her put into bed.' Only then did he return to continue the discussion – while preparing to operate on the next patient. It was quite obvious that with Rupert, his patient came first. 'He cared about people – people meant a great deal to him, and he gave himself to them.'

He noticed people's characteristics, too. The elderly Javanese nurse who was in control of the outpatients department reminded him of the cook in *Alice in Wonderland*, he said, 'though she was much too kindly to pepper the baby! But the way she ordered the patients about! She spoke in Javanese which we, perhaps fortunately, could not understand.'

As in Lanchow years before, he observed the detrimental effects of eating polished rice as compared with the unpolished variety, but his exhortations to switch from one to the other were

to no avail. 'We are not going to eat what the
army eats,' he was told, and that was the end
of it. So, the army flourished on the unpolished
rice, rich with Vitamin B, while the civilians' dis-
carded rice polishings were fed to the ponies that
pulled the dog-carts used for public transport. 'It
was notable how sprightly these ponies were on
their diet, with supplements of bran and molas-
ses from the sugar mills.' As for the patients
who came to the hospital, they got their vitamins
another way. 'We had a male nurse who did a bit
of simple laboratory work, and a lot of injections.
No patient reckoned that the treatment had been
properly started without an injection – which was
almost invariably a Vitamin B complex . . .'

* * *

Although not many of the people of Java were
fanatical Muslims, and it was usually possible
for those who became Christians to live peaceably
in their villages, there was one man whose new-
found faith aroused intense hostility in a member
of his community. As his antagonist was one who
controlled the irrigation water supply, he was in
real difficulty when he discovered that no water
was reaching his fields. However, it was a case
of his extremity proving to be God's opportunity.
In answer to his prayer, publicly expressed, rain
came on his fields, in which he sowed not only
rice, but baby mud-fish, and tomato seedlings
round the edges. When harvest time came his
rice produced a rich crop, the tomatoes were so
plentiful he was able to give some to the whole

village, and when the water was drained off he caught over 150 fish.

The exact number, he reported, was 153.

'I don't suppose he had ever read John 21, verse eleven,' wrote Rupert. 'I never heard whether the irrigation officer was impressed, but certainly the visiting pastor was. He was able to use the experience to show that it is no vain thing to call God "Father".'

For Rupert the incident provided yet another illustration of his favourite theme – the faithfulness of God. It was one on which he often spoke, and as all those who knew him best realised, it was Rupert's unfailing confidence in God's faithfulness that was the key-note of his life.

* * *

When the time came for the Clarkes to leave for furlough, they felt themselves to be in sufficiently good health to break their journey back to England at Damascus, to visit the Holy Land. 'We greatly enjoyed it, but vowed that if we had another opportunity we would do it with a tour group, which we reckoned would be much more economical and instructive.' Then they proceeded to Lingfield in Surrey, to stay with an aunt of Rupert's – from which centre they would have ample opportunity to see Humphrey during school holidays and half-terms. Several weeks therefore elapsed before going for the medical check-up required of all OMF members returning from their fields of service. Only then was it discovered that the deafness of which

Jeannette had been conscious over recent months was due to a tumour growing on the auditory nerve inside the skull.

It came as a shock, and for Jeannette herself it meant a permanent change in her physical condition. The tumour was successfully removed, but it had already involved the nerve which controls the face muscles. As she was recovering from the operation it was with the unpleasant realisation, as she looked into the mirror, that she presented a lop-sided appearance. And although a nerve-astomosis operation improved it, she was now completely deaf in one ear, and her balance was affected.

Meanwhile, they were faced with yet another problem which threatened to prevent them from returning to Java. It was Humphrey's future. He was at school-leaving age by this time, and if they were far away in Indonesia, where could he make his home? It was no easier to think of leaving him alone as a teenager than it had been to face leaving him as a child in boarding school. In some ways it was worse, for all the time he was in 'Chefoo', the school for missionaries' children in the jungle in Malaysia, they knew he was thoroughly happy. The weekly letters he wrote in response to the even more frequent ones they sent to him, assured them of that. And when he had to complete his schooling in England, the hostel for missionaries' children was the place to which he went and felt completely at home. But school days were over, and he was no longer eligible for the hostel. So where would he have a base?

Not that Humphrey himself brought any pressure on bear on them to stay in England.

'Why aren't you going back to Java?' he asked once or twice, adding, 'I don't want you to stay behind for my sake.' His own ambition, as a child, had been to be a missionary doctor like his father. But by the time he took his 'O' levels he had faced the fact that biology was not in his line. He failed in the subject, and his thoughts turned to engineering, and the profession of his forebears – the Army. He would go to Sandhurst. But meanwhile, schooldays over, he was 'fed up with study', and wanted a change.

It came to him indirectly, through his mother, who had friends (one of whom she had known since her nurse training days in Edinburgh) living in the Isle of Wight. Their hospitable home in Newport, a quaint, octagonal building known as the Round House, was one in which Jeannette and Rupert always spent holidays when in England on furlough. And when a sailing centre run by Christians was established near their home, they supported it with enthusiasm. It proved an ideal place for Humphrey to get the change from school life and study for which he was longing. He stayed there for six months before entering Sandhurst, and by that time he had so endeared himself to his hosts, that they suggested he should regard it as his home.

'With that problem sorted out, and Jeannette being fit enough to return to Java, we were able to go back and continue to serve in the Salvation

Army hospital,' wrote Rupert, adding his observations of changed conditions in the country.

'It was interesting to see how the improvement in the economy was soaking down to grass-root level, with the better-off farmers now getting around on motor-cycles; trains running to Jakarta on time, and with their air conditioning functioning reliably ... and with the disorders of prosperity appearing in the local community! Previously we rarely saw hypertension, nor diabetes, but now they were becoming fairly common. And with more motor-cycles there were more traffic accidents, even in the countryside.'

For both Rupert and Jeannette the highlight of the four years which proved to be their last term of service in Java, was the brief holiday they took to return to England for Humphrey's passing out parade from the Army Officers Training College at Sandhurst. (The only time Humphrey ever saw his mother dancing was at the Ball which followed the ceremony!) Then they took him on an unforgettable tour of the Holy Land.

How different so much of it was from what they had seen in 1966! It was in the following year that what has become known as the Six Day War had taken place, when in a lightning attack on her threatening Arab neighbours, Israel had gained possession of the Gaza strip, Sinai, Jordanian territory west of the river Jordan, and a small area of Syria. Now whole tracts of land that had formerly been more or less desert were covered with irrigated orchards, as they pointed out to Humphrey. But it was while they were travelling from Jerusalem towards Galilee that a little incident occurred which Rupert never forgot. They had come to a vast area which evidently particularly impressed Humphrey. After all, he was a soldier now, and modern warfare was what he had been learning about, and had been trained for.

'This plain would be absolutely ideal for a tank battle!' he exclaimed. Rupert gave a little start — he knew where they were.

'This is the plain of Megiddo,' he said, then added rather slowly, 'Where the great battle of Armageddon is expected to take place . . .' Twenty years later, when writing his own memoirs, it was the only conversation held during that holiday that he recorded.

10

A fresh challenge

The years spent in the Salvation Army Hospital in Turen were coming to an end. When the time came for furlough, Rupert realised that even if he were fit enough for another spell there it would be too much for Jeannette, whose health was obviously deteriorating. The pressure of work was revealed in one of her letters home, in which she described a typical day. It started for them at 6 am when drinking their early morning cup of tea they listened for a few minutes to the dawn chorus of the birds – a golden oriole, a scarlet-backed flower-pecker with its clockwork sound, a bulbul with a thrush-like song, and a pair of wren-warblers 'to give us a two-part duet'. But there was little time to enjoy the sights and sounds of beautiful Java.

'It is operating day today. We start out with a list of six, but by lunch time it has lengthened to nine. Home to lunch at 2 pm. Back at 3 pm – finishing off the list at 7.30 pm . . . We have just sat down to our supper when someone comes to ask if Rupert will go and give an injection to a patient with asthma. He is an old friend, and Rupert promises to go as soon as he has finished supper. Bag on bicycle he sets off, and is not home till 9.30 pm. One of the operation cases needs a last visit. And so to bed about 10 pm . . .' But not always without an emergency call. Another entry ran, 'Quietish morning but this pm an emergency operation 750 ccl's of blood re-infused.' As the years passed she admitted, 'It takes us longer to recover from a broken night than it used to.'

By the time 1972 dawned the Salvation Army hospital had its own doctor, and Rupert decided, rather reluctantly, that they must retire from the work and spend some time in England to recuperate.

When on furlough he had usually taken temporary posts in the surgical wards of National Health Service hospitals, but this time he felt that for Jeannette's sake, if not his own, he should try for a long locum in general practice.

'Once again I approached Dr Douglas Johnson, and through him the Lord provided a very suitable post in the beautiful city of Bath. We spent two years there, enjoying the city, the lovely countryside surrounding it, and especially the Christian fellowship of the Widecombe Baptist Church. I could attend even when on call at the weekends, as the vestry telephone had a small repeating light under the gallery, so one could be called for emergencies.'

And, of course, they walked. Walking was an indispensable part of Rupert's programme. That had been evident from the time when, crossing the Atlantic en route for the first time to China, he had urged his reluctant fellow passengers to stride round the deck each day, no matter how high were the waves. He knew exactly how many times back and forth would complete a mile, two miles, three miles . . . They needed the exercise, he told them.

Thirty years later he still held the same views, and fortunately for him, Jeannette agreed with him.

'So when we had holidays we walked some more of the Pennine Way, staying the night at youth hostels with a good many other "mature youths."' Then he added, 'By 1974 Jeannette was in much better health and we were thinking and praying about the onward way when I was again offered a partnership in general practice.'

The offer was a tempting one. They had settled very happily in Bath, they were near retiring age, and there were no immediate openings for Rupert's medical skills in either of their former fields of service, China or Java. They were too old to start learning another language, and altogether, on the face of it, the offer could have been interpreted as being the answer to their prayers.

But the obvious and easy way is not always the right way. Everything in their circumstances encouraged them to settle down, but there was something that proved more powerful and compelling than mere circumstances. Reviewing that period many years later, Rupert summarised it very briefly as 'the word of the Lord'.

It had come to him before, and it came to him

again, though in what way he did not reveal. It may have been through what he was reading, it may have been through a memory, it may have been by an indefinable inner conviction. By whatever means the word came there was no doubt in his mind, or in Jeannette's either, that it was the word of the Lord to them at this time.

'He that putteth his hand to the plough, and looks back, is not fit for the Kingdom of Heaven.' It left no room for speculation as to whether they should remain in Bath. The furrow to be dug with the plough to which they had put their hand lay elsewhere, and they knew in which direction.

'And so we prepared to quit the lovely city, and go back East . . .'

But where?

'Our thoughts and prayers were turned towards the OMF hospital at Saiburi, in south Thailand, which is only about 100 kilometres from the Malaysian border, and where the majority of people speak a brand of Malay not too far removed from the Indonesian Malay which we already used. We thought it best to enquire "round the grapevine" as to whether our ageing assistance would be welcomed, and received an encouraging reply. But the matter was clinched when we had a letter from Dr John Toop, the medical superintendent at Saiburi, asking whether it would be possible for us to come to help out while their surgeon was on furlough.'

The appointment looked like being a short one, but they had no hesitation in accepting it. They disposed of the furniture and various possessions accumulated during their residence in Bath, but had to delay their flight to Bangkok for family reasons. Humphrey was getting married! The Isle of Wight had not only provided him with a home base during his parents' absence but with a bride as well. He had met her at the Christian Sailing Centre, and the wedding was arranged so that Rupert and Jeannette could attend before they set off again for the East.

'It was a very blessed occasion,' wrote Rupert, adding, 'and an opportunity to offload our excellent furlough car on the newly-weds – but then on to exchange the crispness of English winter with the steamy heat of Bangkok, with its noise, its dirt, and its overcrowding.'

The sharp contrast was not only in the weather. They exchanged a settled professional life in an elegant city for a nomadic sort of existence, living out of suitcases in a country where they could not speak the language. It was several weeks before they eventually arrived at their destination, due to floods in the area. During this time of waiting they went to Huahin, a holiday resort south of Bangkok, to stay in a guest house there.

'We had understood it was booked full, but in actual fact it was standing empty, except for various wild cats and snakes. We spent a very useful time of tropical re-acclimatization there, starting with the elimination of five cats and three vipers – all having to be done at night, owing to the Buddhist prejudice against all life-taking, although the murder rate in Thailand is surprisingly high. After this we turned to household repairs and redecorating, and were just getting into our stride when news came through that the airport in Pattani (the capital of the county in which Saiburi is situated) was again open. So we returned to Bangkok, and took the plane to Pattani, where we were welcomed by some of the missionaries, including Dorothy Jupp, an old friend from north-west China days. She was to have been Jeannette's senior missionary in Ningsia – but I took over that job!' A fifty kilometer ride in the hospital mini van brought them to their destination.

* * *

During the period when Rupert was under house arrest on the Tibetan border, four of his fellow missionaries were settling in, feeling somewhat confused, in the unaccustomed climate and conditions of the tropics. They had been working among Muslims in north-west China, and that door having been decisively closed under Communism, had now been designated to pioneer work among Muslims in the four southern provinces of Thailand.

Their way had been fraught with difficulties – not but that the Thai officials were always polite and charming, while some of the Chinese, Indian and Pakistanis thinly scattered in the towns actually spoke a little English, to the great relief of the four middle-aged westerners whose crash course in the Thai language was proving sadly inadequate when it came to everyday conversation. No, their difficulties of what is commonly known as 'culture shock' were as nothing compared with the problem of locating the very people they had been sent to evangelize.

The Malays, they had been told, comprised 80% of the population in these southern provinces – but where were they to be found? They evidently all lived out of town, mysteriously melting away after marketing or visiting the mosque, into the jungles and plantations that stretched away into the mountains as far as the eye could see. They were as elusive as the Muslims of north-west China had proved, though their women were obviously freer, moving about the streets in colourful sarongs, unlike their dark-robed sisters who were confined in walled compounds. Their vendors of fruit and dried fish, rice and squawking fowls might flood the markets and crowd the buses till the town seemed full of them, but when it came to house-to-house visiting, they simply were not there. They lived out of town, scattered in their little *kampongs* in the thickly wooded countryside, difficult to find, and although friendly, clinging tenaciously to their own language, their own culture, and above all, their own religion. And although most of them were easy-going, knowing little and caring less about politics, there were those among them who bitterly resented their Thai overlords, asserting that the four southern provinces rightly belonged to the Malay people and forming themselves into rebel bands lurking in the jungle-clad mountains bordering on Malaysia, a Muslim country.

Not that they were the only law-breakers who found the jungle a convenient centre for their activities. There were the big business smugglers who had ways and means of getting contraband goods across the border for purely mercenary motives. There were the individuals who had something to gain and nothing to lose by doing the dirty work connected with these enterprises. And there were those who took advantage of the general unrest to augment their incomes by a little skilful banditry here and there.

To go out into the jungle seeking Malays whose language they could not even speak was obviously out of the question, particularly as the majority of the South Thailand team were women. Instead, a means must be devised to bring the Malays in, and talks with Thai officials revealed that a medical service for the rural areas would be acceptable. It was not required in the larger towns, where the government already had its hospitals, but in Saiburi, a fishing port on the east coast, it would meet a need. So the open-fronted shop there, which Dorothy Jupp and her younger colleague had turned into a guest room lined with Bible pictures and Scripture verses became the Saiburi Christian Clinic, with a doctor in attendance. And that was only a beginning. By 1960 a forty-bed hospital had been built by a lagoon, on a strip of land lying between two graveyards – the Chinese and the Malay. The dreary sand dunes in this somewhat dismal spot had been transformed by the time the Clarkes arrived, and Rupert enthusiastically described it as 'an oasis of flowering trees and green lawns, having a never-failing well which not only supplies water for the hospital, but has enough left over to sprinkle the lawns in the dry season'.

The surroundings to which they had come were
pleasant, their colleagues congenial, and since
the Thai government regulations required three
doctors for the forty-bed hospital, the pressure
of work would obviously be much lighter than
it had been either on the Tibetan border or in
Java. But they found that there was a cloud over
the whole missionary community, and they knew
what caused it. A special daily prayer meeting
was held exclusively for two of their colleagues,
whose names were mentioned urgently, sometimes brokenly.

'Minka and Margaret.'

Somewhere out in the jungle-clad mountains
Minka and Margaret were being held in captiv-
ity, and no-one knew where they were.

Months before, the abduction of two nurses
from a rural clinic for leprosy sufferers in south
Thailand had made headline news. Although
kidnappings, murders, hold-ups and gun-battles
between the military police and the bandits had
been going on for years in the troubled provinces
on the Malaysian border, it was the first time two
westerners had been abducted.

'Two women missionaries kidnapped by
bandits!'
'Malay terrorists capture missionary nurses!'
'Welsh nurse and Dutch companion abducted
in south Thailand!'

The news media got on to the story so quickly
that the embassies and OMF had difficulty in

getting the information to the relatives before they heard it over the air. That was back in April 1974, and after a time the news media had nothing else to report. But during the months that had elapsed, negotiations for their release had been going on between the OMF superintendent of South Thailand, Ian Murray, and the kidnappers, carried on through mysterious intermediaries, and involving him in some precarious situations himself. But the outcome of them all, while resulting in a few items, including a Bible, being conveyed to the nurses, and two or three very carefully worded letters being received from them, the negotiations ended in a stalemate.

The guerillas made two demands, neither of which could be met.

The first one was the payment of ransom money. The fact that it was so high as to be virtually impossible to pay was not the reason for its refusal. Once holding missionaries for ransom was seen to be a profitable business every other missionary (and missionary child) would be at risk. It had long been the expressed policy of the OMF. that in the event of a kidnapping, no ransom money would be paid.

The second demand was even more disturbing. It was that the Overseas Missionary Fellowship should write officially, protesting against Israeli action in connection with the Palestinian people. Suddenly there came the realisation that the Fellowship was in danger of becoming unwittingly involved in international politics. There could be no question of being caught up in the explosive situation between Israel and the Arabs, one way or the other. So both demands were refused, and the two nurses remained in guerilla hide-outs in the jungle. No communications had been received from them for months by the time the Clarkes arrived in Saiburi, though rumours were not lacking, some encouraging, some the reverse. It was not until March 1975, that the news flashed round the world that two bodies had been found in the jungle in south Thailand, believed to be the missionaries abducted by bandits last year . . .

John Toop, tuning in as usual to the BBC at 7 am listened in stunned silence, then darted into action. He had to find out – a quick motor-cycle ride to the provincial capital, to the police there. A few hours later he returned, his face grave. Yes, it was true. There was no doubt about it. Items found on the unrecognisable bodies, now only bones, proved that they were all that remained of Minka and Margaret – and that they had been shot through the back of the head about six months ago.

Shot through the back of the head. It was the very form of execution that Rupert had anticipated for himself when the situation had become particularly threatening years before on the Tibetan border. Well, at any rate, it was swift and painless, and they had been together . . . But the sense of loss and disappointment went very deep, especially for those who had been praying for the Lord's name to be vindicated in their release. 'I was hard put to defend my faith in God – it took me a full day to get over the disappointment I felt,' said one, while another confessed to facing many conflicting thoughts and questions. Nor was it only the missionary body that felt it. One of the leprosy patients wrote most movingly to the two mothers telling what he felt as he thought of them.

> . . . It makes me feel sick at heart, as though something has pierced my heart and got stuck there. When I go to my rest, alone as always, I cannot help but think of them. Then I see the face of Minka who was always smiling, and as for Margaret, crossing the muddy rice fields to have communion with the family at Nongjig. My tears flow and then I go to sleep.
> Love and highest respects,
> Jit.

It was a little child who struck an entirely different note. On hearing the news he went to his mother and enquired eagerly, 'Mummy, is Auntie Minka in Jesus' house now?' He was not worried about what appeared to others to be unanswered prayer. He had been praying for Auntie Minka, and now she was safe and happy in heaven! What could be better? As Rupert, with characteristic brevity, expressed it,
'Released – into the arms of Jesus!'

* * *

Meanwhile, whatever might have been the private emotions and questionings of the hospital team, the work continued as usual, and for the Clarkes, Rupert in particular, life was full and varied. Of primary importance was the preparation for an examination which must be passed before he could practice in Thailand at all. This was required of all foreign-trained doctors.

'The straightforward medicine and surgery was no great problem, but biochemistry and suchlike had altered a lot in the forty years since I had learned it, and I had forgotten a lot anyway.' In addition, visits to Bangkok were necessary to deal with visa regulations, inspection of damaged luggage, etc. 'I got to know the railway to Bangkok pretty well, with five visits in the first three months. However, there was no great hardship in the journey, as the State railway provides quite comfortable Japanese-built sleeping coaches, with air-conditioning available at little extra cost. The trip of over 1,000 kilometres passed quite well, in about twenty hours.'

And the railway journeys always had an added interest for him – the engine. While waiting to board the train he would stroll up and have a look at it, and reported that the express trains were hauled by diesel-electric engines 'of various origins'. And he noticed that when the price of oil suddenly rocketed, there was considerable discussion about re-installing 'the trusty old Krupp wood-burners, which could use up the overage timber from the rubber plantations'. Perhaps it was not without a passing sense of regret that when the price of oil fell again he saw the old steam engines left to rust on sidings!

There was more enforced travelling for them both when their visitors visas expired and they had to leave Thailand for a stay of indefinite duration in the OMF home in Kuala Lumpur, Malaysia. They were there for several weeks, trying to gain an understanding of the Thai language with the use of Thai tapes, but eventually news came through that Rupert had passed the medical exam.

'So when we learned that I was now a doctor, we set off on the homeward trail.' Returning to Bangkok to complete formalities, they eventually arrived back in Saiburi – but not without a road accident which might have proved disastrous. They were speeding along the highway in Malaysia in a Mini, when suddenly one of the tyres burst, resulting in the car landing upside down on the verge on the opposite side of the road. Providentially, there were no other vehicles on that part of the road at that moment. 'The Lord graciously arranged a gap in the busy traffic,' was the way Rupert reported the incident, and went on to explain how they got going again. 'The first vehicle to pull up was a timber-carrier, whose Chinese loggers quickly righted the Mini, and whilst two lifted the back another changed the tyre, then well-wished us on our way.'

A few months later he could have lost his life by drowning, but for another providential 'arrangement'. He was in the habit of swimming in the estuary of the Saiburi river once or twice a week. It was free of the jellyfish which are hazards of sea bathing in those parts, and there were no sharks, either. But on one occasion he misjudged the tide, and the strength of the river current, and found himself swept out to sea for about half a mile. He started swimming steadily towards

the shore, but realized that he was making practically no headway. 'Then I had some doubt as
to whether my coronary arteries would stand up
to the strain indefinitely . . .'

No-one on the shore would be on the lookout
for him, he knew. He was a powerful and experienced swimmer, and there would be no reason for
anyone to be concerned about him at this stage.
And by the time his non-appearance had resulted
in a search party launching out for him it would
be dark . . . He dared not stop swimming, but the
shore seemed as far away as ever, and his heart
was pumping.

What he did not know until later was that a
small Malay boy had been watching him from the
shore, and saw when he was swept out to sea. The
child went and told his fisherman father, and so
it came about that when Rupert was conscious
of weakening he heard a shout, a fishing boat
loomed into sight and sturdy arms were stretched
out to pull him aboard. Some would have termed
it a lucky coincidence that the child 'happened'
to be watching Rupert, but he himself did not see
it in that way. 'Thanks be to God for causing the
little boy to see me,' was the way he put it. On
such apparently coincidental 'happenings' hang
the issues of life and death more often than most
of us realise.

The Christian hospital in Saiburi had already
gained a good reputation in the neighbourhood,
with its succession of good doctors and surgeons,
so that people wounded by gun-shot or traffic
accidents, as well as ordinary surgical cases were
brought along with confidence. 'A few of them

did receive general anaesthetics, but almost all the routine surgery was still performed under some form of area analgesia.' And Rupert, ever eager to simplify and economise, switched from using expensive gut to nylon fishing line. The hospital administration ran into difficulties over the matter of blood transfusion, though.

'The predominately Malay population, as a whole, were reluctant to give blood for transfusion, but most of the trishaw pedallers were very ready to sell their blood for that purpose – but at an exorbitant price. Then, when we presented our very moderate bill to the patient the family would be unable to pay, as they had used up all their money on bought blood. However, by a policy of non-transfusion we were able to bring the price down to a reasonable figure. I well remember one Malay man who brought in his wife for operation, and who refused even to have his blood tested for compatibility saying, "I can easily buy another wife".

'And yet I suppose he prayed five times a day to Allah the Compassionate!' added Rupert indignantly. He did not divulge what he said to the man – probably not much. He could get his point across with the use of very few words.

The dangers of the neighbourhood in which they lived were frequently brought home to the missionaries by the arrival of border police suffering from wounds inflicted by the guerillas. In these cases there was never any difficulty about blood transfusions. The Chief of Police apparently had a computer-like memory in which were stored the blood groups of all the men under his

control, and he simply announced who was going
to donate the needed blood – and that was all
there was to it.

Although living conditions and diet (which was
mainly composed of fish and rice) were different
from those in either Java or China, there was
one great advantage in Saiburi which was reminiscent of the old days in Lanchow. It was the
complete freedom to preach the Gospel. Just as
before the Communist takeover in China preaching had been unrestricted in Christian hospitals,
so now in Saiburi the situation was the same.
Each morning in the out-patients waiting area
the hospital evangelists preached in both Thai
and Malay, and the public address system carried the messages to the wards. In the afternoons
there would be preaching in the wards as well,
and on Sunday afternoons the doctors themselves preached, with Rupert taking his turn.
'As many patients understood standard Malay
– from watching Malaysia TV – they were better
able to understand my brand of Malay. In later
years we had TV screens installed, and were able
to show some excellent video tapes, including the
much-appreciated "Jesus" film.'

In May 1977, Rupert and Jeannette decided
to take a holiday to visit Humphrey and his
family in the celebrated German city of Hameln
(Hamlin) where he was stationed. They were
both apparently in good health when they set
off, and planned to be back in Saiburi in July,
six weeks later. It proved to be their last holiday
together.

11

End of an era

'What a lovely wedding dress!' exclaimed Jeannette, inspecting the lace, fondling the soft material, then laughingly holding it up against herself to get the full effect. She smiled across at Helen and admitted rather wistfully, 'I'd have loved to be married in a wedding dress!' No chance of that in Lanchow!

It was the first time that she had had the opportunity to get to know her daughter-in-law. She and Rupert had met her briefly, shortly after Humphrey had become engaged, then again at the wedding, but now at last they were actually all living together as a family, and Jeannette was obviously in her element. She loved the two children, especially baby Daniel. 'I'd wanted another baby so badly,' she confided to Helen, and constituted herself as nurse to her little grandson, bathing him, dressing him, cuddling him. He was small enough to lie very contentedly in her arms, looking up at her and smiling as she talked to him.

Watching her, Humphrey and Helen sensed

the fulfilment of a deep desire in her for simple
family life, and realized she would have been
glad to retire now from the inevitable strain of
a mission hospital. She was prepared to accept it
unconditionally as long as Rupert was fit for it,
and obviously he was, but for these few weeks she
could relax and indulge her natural tendencies.
British Army quarters in Hameln were in the
best position in the city, right on the edge of a
wood, ideal for walking, or just strolling with the
baby. And after a few days there they all moved
on together to fulfil another of her desires. She
had sometimes mentioned how much she would
like to go camping in Austria, and Humphrey
and Helen, planning their own holiday, had
arranged it with that in mind. They would all
go to Austria.

Not everything went quite smoothly. The wheel
bearings of the trailer carrying their baggage and
tent equipment gave way as they were nearing
Nuremberg late one Saturday. There was no way
of getting repairs done at that hour, so in the
pouring rain Rupert and Humphrey put up the
tent and they all spent a rather wet weekend in
it. But things were righted on Monday morning,
and they went on to Nuremberg where Jeannette
decided to display her prowess at cooking 'in the
field'. She constructed a primitive stove from cake
tins, and proceeded to bake an enormous batch
of scones. Helen was very impressed, if a little
disconcerted when the scones kept coming too
quickly and profusely for appetites to keep up
with them.

She was impressed in other ways, too. After they

left Vienna the wind and the rain caught up with
them again, and pitching the tents by the Austrian
lake was no easy matter. But Jeannette insisted
on the small tent she and Rupert were to sleep
in being erected first. 'Helen and the children can
get in there and keep dry,' she said. Daniel must
be fed and changed, whatever happened!

The days by the beautiful lake with mountains in the distance passed very happily, and
if Jeannette was feeling a little discomfort she
kept it to herself until about three days before
they were due to return, when she admitted that
she was having abdominal pains, and they were
getting worse.

Rupert, calm as usual, examined her, could find
no obvious cause for the trouble, and said, 'I think
we'd better postpone our return to Thailand, and
book a flight to London instead. We'll go to the
Mildmay Mission Hospital and see what they can
do for us'.

The Mildmay Mission Hospital near Shoreditch
Church in the east end of London was a familiar
haven for many missionaries. They went there
for their medical check-ups when home on furlough, and Rupert himself had worked there for a
short time years before. Jeannette was promptly
admitted for investigation, and an exploratory
operation was pronounced necessary. It disclosed
irremovable cancer.

* * *

It is not easy to describe the effect on the emotions
of devastating personal news. Neither Rupert nor

Jeannette had expected her condition to be as serious as it proved to be, and it came as a shock to realize that within a matter of months, even weeks, her life would end. Writing of the experience years later Rupert was able to reveal how they had reacted – and he condensed it into one sentence.

'We wept a bit, but decided that the Lord really is Master of all.'

'We wept a bit . . .' They had loved each other, lived, worked, endured and aspired together for more than thirty years. Now they must be parted, and Rupert go on in life without her.

They wept. He acknowledged it. But over and beyond the natural grief their confidence in the sovereignty of their God and his purposes for them prevailed. Their Master was in control – and everything he did was for the best. After a couple of weeks her condition had improved sufficiently for her to be moved down to the hospital's convalescence home in Worthing, where she was able to take some short walks by the seaside. But then the trouble recurred, and she was re-admitted into the Mildmay Mission Hospital for terminal care.

Rupert visited her every day, and stayed with her for most of it. 'We would start with the reading from "Daily Light" and prayer, and then spend much of the rest of the day reading and talking. As she grew weaker she preferred light fare, and we re-read many of Arthur Ransome's *Swallows and Amazons* series which had delighted Humphrey as a boy – and which still delight me!

'When Jeannette's condition was obviously deteriorating rapidly I followed Humphrey's instructions and went along to Bethnal Green police station about 10.30 one morning, to ask them to contact the Ministry of Defence to obtain compassionate leave for him. The police checked with the hospital as to the truth of the story, telephoned the MOD and they contacted Humphrey's unit in Hameln. He was out on an exercise, but they had him collected, emplaned, and landed in England by 2.30 pm. . . .' Humphrey had told him that the Army knows how to communicate fast. Rupert was in a position to endorse it after that.

They spent hours every day by her bedside, in a quiet, unhurried intimacy that had started long before, when Humphrey was still a child. The apparently trivial incident when sitting beside his mother he had sung 'Come into my heart, Lord Jesus' had laid the foundation for it. When the time came for him to be parted from them and go to boarding school he had accepted the separation as being necessary 'so that other little boys and girls can know about Jesus'. And through all those years, as he grew to boyhood, and to manhood, their letters to him had been the vital communication between them. They had both written to him every week – Sunday afternoon's regular occupation had been 'writing to Humph'. Two separate letters were placed in one envelope and dispatched by air.

Jeannette had usually written another letter some time during the week. Her letters were less methodical and factual than Rupert's, but delightfully illustrated with sketches of scenes and incidents she had witnessed – a duck man shepherding his flock of ducks, little boys wearing funny hats, an ox-cart passing along the road. Peppered with little bits of information, too.

When he had been able to go and actually live with them during holidays, in the hospital in Java, it had been like coming home, he knew so much about it. How proud he had been to go with his father into the wards, how satisfying it had been to see for himself the people and places his mother had described so vividly. And when the time came for him to leave the congenial atmosphere of the Chefoo school for missionaries' children in Malaysia, and go to prep school in England, those letters had been even more of a lifeline in what was for him an unhappy period. All through the difficult teenage years those letters had come unfailingly, keeping him in touch with the meaningful world in which his parents lived.

He wondered, as he sat quietly in the ward in the Mildmay Mission Hospital what anxieties had oppressed his mother when there was uncertainty as to whether he would 'make the grade' academically, and what would happen if he didn't. He marvelled at the way things had worked out and how, in spite of being regarded as being of poor intellectual ability, he had surprised his teachers by doing well in the 11+ exam, and later passing the entrance exam to St Lawrence Senior School.

He marvelled, too, at the way things were working out in little personal relationships. With a son's insight he had perceived that his mother was sometimes disappointed that Rupert did not express his affection in words and actions that she would have appreciated. But in those last weeks of her life his love was expressed in deeds. His travelling day after day from North Finchley, where he was staying with Helen's parents, to do nothing else but sit by her, spoke more clearly than any words.

And the timing of events, too. Rupert was still alert, strong, and his surgical work was his life. He was fit and eager to fulfil what he believed to be his calling – a doctor on the mission field. But Jeannette's work was over, and she ready to relinquish her hold on life.

'What does it feel like, Mum, to know that you are going?' Humphrey and Helen asked her once, and they never forgot her reply.

'Oh, it's just Goodbye here, and Hello there,' she said as easily as if she were off for a visit to friends. Then she added revealingly,

'And I haven't got to pack a suitcase!' She had done so much packing and moving in her life – now it was over. She had run her race, finished her course, and was ready to pass on.

It was very quiet in the ward that 22 September, as those sitting watching her saw that she had stopped breathing. 'Goodbye here . . .' But Rupert and Humphrey knew that was not the end of it.

'. . . Hello there!'

And the trumpets were sounding for her on the other side.

* * *

Rupert returned to Saiburi early in October, and
as he expressed it, found plenty of work to keep
his mind occupied until one Monday afternoon in
January, when he was jerked out of his routine.
He was in the out-patients clinic and a messenger
came hurrying in with a telegram addressed to
him. It was an urgent request from headquarters
for him to transfer as soon as possible to the
OMF hospital in Manorom, central Thailand. No
explanation was given.

To transfer – that meant more than a brief
visit. He discussed it with his colleagues, and
they all agreed that he had better go immediately. 'Probably the visas of one of the surgeons
has run out, and they haven't been able to renew
it.' With a re-arrangement of duties they would
manage without him, so application was made
to the Thai government office in Pattani for
permission to transfer. Permission was granted
the following day, an air ticket to Bangkok purchased, and early on Wednesday morning he was
waiting for the bus to take him to the air field
when someone arrived rather breathlessly with
news that another telegram had been received. It
enlarged on the first one, and contained stagger-
ingly bad news from Manorom. There had been
a terrible road accident. A lorry with a drunken
driver had crashed head on into the hospital
minibus containing a party of missionaries and
their children. They had been for a picnic and
were on their way home when it happened.
Among the twelve who were killed outright were
the two surgeons, Ian Gordon-Smith and Noel
Sampson.

Two surgeons killed, and Dr Julia Brown seriously injured. And Rupert knew that Dr John Townsend, the medical superintendent of Manorom, was home in England on furlough. Over and above the stunning shock for the whole community, there would be the sudden responsibility for those who found themselves without warning in charge of patients needing attention, awaiting operations . . . They would need all the support he could give, and he was glad he had not delayed to respond to the summons to proceed to Manorom as quickly as possible. He arrived there on Wednesday evening – and to his amazement he found that John Townsend was there already.

'He had learned of the accident on the Saturday evening BBC news broadcast, to which none of us in Saiburi happened to have listened.

'He had forthwith applied to the Liverpool police, who had arranged for a visa to be available at the Thai consulate in London on Sunday morning. Someone else had acquired an air ticket for him, and he was on his way back to Thailand on Sunday afternoon. By the time I reached Manorom he was well back on the job. In fact, he was back before news of the accident had even reached us in the south.'

This was not the first time that members of the OMF had met with violent deaths in the little country of Thailand. Lilian Hamer and Roy Orpin had both been murdered in the tribal areas in the north, only a few years after all the missionaries had been withdrawn from China. Dorothy Woodward was killed in a bus crash. Minka and Margaret had been assassinated by the Malay terrorists. Now a drunken Thai driver had killed outright five missionaries and seven children.

As far as Rupert himself was concerned he was especially distressed to learn that Mrs Parry and two of her three children were among the dead. Mrs Parry – he had known her years ago on the Tibetan border as 'Twink', the little daughter of Norman and Amy Macintosh. What a shock it must have been for them to hear the news. And they were not the only ones who were mourning the loss of those they loved. It was a very subdued group that welcomed Rupert into their midst, but they were thankful to see him. The work of the hospital had to go on, and they needed his surgical skills. His knowledge of the Thai language was inadequate, but with English speaking nurses in the wards he could make himself understood, while in the out-patients department his interpreter was a Thai-Chinese aide to whom he could speak in Mandarin.

'My stay in Central Thailand was for about a year,' he wrote adding, 'And a very happy one at that. The surgical set-up was much more sophisticated than ours in the south, and with very good general anaesthetics available. A high standard had been set by Mr Ian Gordon-Smith (who had been driving the minibus) and his colleagues.' Then he went on to note the differences between south and central Thailand, especially from a medical point of view.

'One thing that struck me most forcibly was

the large number of road accidents, which were largely due to the alcoholism of the Thai drivers in the central area, as opposed to the nonalcoholic Muslim drivers of the south.

'Another thing was that many fractures were treated at Manorom, whilst in the south almost all fractures were treated by the village bonesetters. Some of their results were a bit oldfashioned anatomically but at least they almost always obtained bony union, and that in a shorter time than we could. Our own radiographer broke his thigh, and we reckoned that he would be off work for at least three months; but the bone-setter sent him back to work in six weeks, walking with only a slight limp. I think that they, as well as the Chinese bone-setters, use some herbal substance which speeds up union – but I was never able to discover this wellkept secret!

'There was a great difference also in the prevalence of stomach and duodenal ulcers. In Saiburi we could only spot one about every two months, while in Manorom there were often three or four ward patients who were either bleeding from, or recovering from perforation of their peptic ulcers. I don't think that the diet is very different, despite the predominance of the Malay race in the south, so perhaps it is a racial difference.

'The climate in Manorom was not so nice as at Saiburi, where the land and sea breezes kept us at a fairly even 85 Fahrenheit all the year round. At Manorom the weather was very hot and sticky, and the cool weather called for woollies, whilst one treated the coughs, colds and pneumonias of the ill-clad local people, living in very draughty houses.'

If the climate at Manorom compared unfavourably with that at Saiburi, the political climate was definitely better. There was no fear of rebels or terrorists in the neighbourhood, so 'it was possible to take long walks each week – usually about fifteen miles in a circle hinged upon the bank of the great Chaophrya River on its way to Bangkok and the sea. The rainy season of 1978 was not heavy, and the river did not flood, but the following year there was ten feet of water in the out-patients department, and patients were delivered by water taxis to the upper storey of the main hospital block.' (Unusually heavy rains had threatened to flood Bangkok even more than usual, so the Government ordered the water board to close all their sluices, flooding the rural areas, rather than submerge the capital.)

Weekly missionary prayer meetings were held at Manorom, and one of them in particular remained one of Rupert's vivid memories.

'It was led by the Malaysian-Chinese nurse, Lily Yeoh, who gave a most moving account of how she came to know Christ whilst training in England. She had completed her training at Hemel Hempstead, and was working in London when she re-visited friends at Hemel Hempstead. Whilst the evening meal was being prepared she picked up a copy of Mark's gospel in modern English, and was so interested that she asked to take it back to London with her. She read it on the Green Line coach, and by the time she had reached Oxford Circus she had also reached the conclusion that she would "follow Jesus." She was doing twelve-hour nursing shifts, but was able to visit neighbouring All Souls Church in Langham Place two or three times. She bought a Bible, and as she read it God spoke to her, and she decided to clear out a lot of books from her book shelf. Later she decided that dancing was wrong for her, and she quit the dance floor, but still stuck to the idea that she would go to Australia and make a lot of money in private nursing. On her way there she visited her home in Malaysia, and discovered to her delight that she no longer needed to live in fear of evil spirits.

'"You westerners don't know what that means to us" she said, for Malaysian Buddhism is largely a matter of keeping the evil spirits at bay.

'She journeyed on to Australia to earn her good money but God had other plans for her . . . After a few months she decided that she no longer wanted to make a lot of money, but that God wanted her to go to Bible College instead – and that was the next step on the way to joining the OMF.

'When she had finished her own story she introduced her two Chinese friends, both of whom had been converted when doing their nursing training overseas, and both were now in "full-time service" for the Lord.'

Rupert concluded his report of that meeting with what was for him an unusual flight of the imagination as he wrote,

'I could picture Dr Hudson Taylor looking

down from heaven, and rejoicing to see Chinese missionaries leading the China Inland Mission prayer meetings!'

There was another occasion which he remembered, too. He was with a group of the Thai nurses and trainees, and was asked to tell them about his time of imprisonment and house arrest in China – 'Chairman Mao's unwilling guest', as he described himself. He spoke in English, and the theatre sister, who had trained at St Thomas' Hospital in London, acted as interpreter. He spoke on his favourite theme, and as he related his experiences during those momentous days when he had nothing to eat but rotting cabbage leaves boiled in water, he saw it as 'a fine opportunity to point the whole staff to "hold the faithfulness of God" as Rotherham translated Mark 11 verse 22.'

Perhaps it was partly due to his long absence from Saiburi that he saw things more objectively, and found himself more and more impressed by the spiritual fruitfulness of work among sufferers from leprosy, that most dreaded disease. He had seen something of the same nature in Lanchow, where a compound in the hospital had been specially reserved for leprosy patients. Many of them, shunned and despised by their own people, had travelled long distances to reach this place of refuge. Among them had been Tibetans and Muslims, as well as Chinese, and some of them, finding at last the love and acceptance denied them elsewhere, had turned to Christ. Christ's compassion for them, revealed through his servants, combined with the faithful proclamation of the Word of God, had achieved what preaching alone had failed to do.

The same thing was happening in south Thailand. He wrote,

'By Christmas 1978 it was possible to return to Saiburi, and I began to take a more active interest in the leprosy wing of the hospital, for from those ten beds have come almost all the Malays who have turned to Christ from Islam. For fifteen years of Gospel preaching there had been no obvious result, but then the break occurred.' Then he went on to relate how it came about.

'Uncle Su-Mat had been a "freedom fighter" in the jungle of the Thai-Malaysian border from his youth upward, but he became so disabled by the leprous ulceration of his fingers and feet that he could neither pull a trigger nor keep up with the squadron in its hasty journeys as they were constantly hunted by the security forces on both sides of the border. So he decided (or perhaps his leader decided for him) that it was time to give up his jungle existence and return to civilisation. He wisely moved to the Thai side of the border, but was deeply depressed, knowing that his disease was incurable, and that as he had killed so many people there was no hope of heaven for him. Although,' Rupert added as a sort of afterthought, 'as I suppose that those would all have been "unbelievers", the Ayatollah Khomeni would have assured him an abundant entrance into an Islamic heaven!

'His fellow villagers persuaded him to attend the clinic in Rodjok where he was amazed to find educated and refined missionary nurses cleaning up his stinking, ulcerated feet. It was a job assigned to the lowest of the low in Thai society (as it would appear to have been in the Israeli society of the time of Jesus). As he continued to attend the clinic he saw more of the life of Christ in the two clinic nurses, and understood more of the Gospel preached there, and he determined that he, too, would be Christ's man – cost what it may. He and a friend were the first to be baptised into Christ from Islam in South Thailand.'

The seed of the Malay Church in South Thailand had been sown deep – for the two clinic nurses who tended Su Mat's feet, and led him to Christ, were Minka and Margaret. When it was known that they were captured, he and his friend offered their lives in exchange for the two nurses, but not surprisingly their offer was scorned. 'The bandit chief was not interested in "mere lepers".

'Now there are about fifty baptised Malays, almost all from the leprosy work, and Su Mat, though severely handicapped, has become the leader of the Malay language church in Saiburi. It is amazing to see how he manages to turn the leaves of the New Testament with only the stumps of a few insensitive fingers . . .' But in practical matters things did not go particularly easily for Su-Mat, Rupert observed, and he continued,

'Paul the apostle, who spent some years of his early life persecuting the Christian believers, and seems to have been foremost in arranging the martyrdom of Stephen, spent much of his later life being persecuted and near-murdered himself . . . Likewise Su-Mat, who had killed so many people as a "freedom fighter" has also had a very harrassed time as a sin-forgiven follower of Jesus . . .

'Maybe these jagged-edged people need to be knocked about a bit to make them into beautiful building blocks for the temple of God.' Then he added,

'But it's a painful process!'

12

The furrow completed

'We are sometimes asked if we pray for, expect, and see miraculous healing, and I think that, on the whole, we don't', Rupert wrote once, and made no apology for it. He believed that the training and skill he had received were God-given, and that through them the work of healing would be done. 'But sometimes, usually when we are at our wits' end, we do pray for it, expect it, and see it', and he went on to cite two cases in which there was no other explanation but that God had intervened.

'Two weeks ago an old Thai-Chinese man was dying from kidney failure following a prostatectomy which I had performed, and which had been followed by most of the known complications! But when we prayed for him at the weekly missionary prayer meeting I remembered that on the shelf in the pharmacy store there were some free samples of a new antibiotic ...' The memory coming so unexpectedly during that time of prayer was promptly followed up, and in a short time the old man was up and about again – and his Mandarin-speaking attendant was discussing and reading the Chinese Bible to him.

Then there was the case of the young woman who had been unconscious from cerebral malaria for a week. 'She seemed to be sinking steadily until it was decided to pray for her in the presence of her parents, and as the party went along to the ward for that purpose, the lass sat up in bed and began to talk!'

But medical work among the Malays seemed mainly with leprosy cases, and writing in 1980 Rupert reported that although about two thousand patients were under treatment, they were well aware that many more sufferers were in the hamlets and villages hidden away in the jungle. The difficulties and dangers of finding them were still too great to be undertaken lightly, and there were setbacks to discourage the workers. The house where one young Dutch nurse was living was broken into when she was alone, and she was attacked, while the motor-cycle of another, who used it to visit the clinics, was stolen. The cycle, as it happened, was very soon recovered by the police, but the culprit himself proved to be the great disappointment.

'To our horror we discovered that it had been stolen by a teenage leprosy lad who had recently been baptised!' The dismay with which this news was received was understandable, but Rupert revealed a surprising depth of insight when he wrote, rather sadly,

'I don't know what can be done to salvage the lad, who has been in trouble with the police before – an orphaned teenager, resentful of discipline, but probably a true believer. Leprosy patients understandably get twists of the psyche, and care for them is always a stressful occupation.' He concluded his letter with the words, 'We wrestle not against flesh and blood – but we have a Mighty Champion on our side.'

If the spiritual difficulties in the work remained the same, by 1983 political and social conditions in south Thailand were improving considerably. By a successful policy of building more roads into the countryside, and establishing schools and clinics there, the Malay guerillas were being pushed further and further back into the jungle. The introduction in rural areas of electricity was particularly important, Rupert observed, for 'now even the humblest bamboo shack sports a television aerial, and the inmates tune in either to Bangkok or Kuala Lumpur programmes. To largely illiterate country dwellers they open a new window on life. Admittedly, a rather materialistic vision, but at any rate pointing to a better life than hiding in the jungle.' And from his personal point of view, there was an added advantage in the changing situation.

'When we arrived it was scarcely safe to venture from the hospital to the village one kilometre away, but before I left it was possible to take quite long walks in the country!' Then he continued,

'A great factor in the improved situation is the yearly visit of the Royal Family to the south. They usually arrive in August and stay for about six weeks, bringing with them a complete hospital team which settles into the Government hospital at Narathiwat, about fifty kilometres south of

Saiburi. There they offer free, and very expert, treatment to all on the King's privy purse. We used to save up all our difficult cases (such as those needing heart surgery), for the Royal visit; and any who could not be treated locally were sent up to the leading hospitals in Bangkok. Likewise, such leprosy cases as were likely to need much hospital care were also sent along, to be accepted graciously into "The Queen's Fund" – to the great relief of our finances.

'On two occasions the Royal Family visited our hospital (the King driving his own Range Rover, wearing an open necked shirt and trainers!) and received enthusiastic welcomes from Thai, Malays and foreigners alike. The people of Thailand are devoted to their King, for while military and political leaders come and go, the King remains the peaceful and beloved head of the nation.

'Not only does His Majesty care for the sick of the south, but he also arranges irrigation schemes and similar projects to the great benefit of the area, for whereas such schemes ordered by the government may *possibly* be implemented, those proposed by the King are carried out swiftly under his personal supervision.'

The visits of the King to the hospital were made in a day, but when the British Consul arrived he remained for the best part of a week. He had been working hard for the release of an English girl who was imprisoned in Bangkok for drug smuggling. The Consul believed that in her innocence, she had been completely unaware that the drugs had been slipped into her luggage by

the man she had trusted. The story of Rita Night-
ingale and her eventual release from prison on
the granting of the King's pardon made headline
news at the time. However, the Consul's visit
to Saiburi was on an entirely different errand,
and one which he did not divulge until later.
Someone had put forward Rupert's name as one
deserving the OBE, and the Consul had come
to see the nominee for himself. Rupert knew
nothing about it, of course, at the time, but
the outcome of the visit was that in 1983 he
found himself at Buckingham Palace, arrayed
in light grey morning dress (by courtesy of Moss
Bros), accompanied by his son and daughter-in-
law, Major and Mrs Humphrey Clarke. It was
a memorable occasion, and one that increased
his inherent respect for royalty – the Queen was
gracious as always, and he had no difficulty in
obeying the Scriptural injunction to give honour
where honour is due.

Shortly after that event he went to the Isle
of Wight for a holiday in the Round House. He
and Jeannette had always spent part of their
furlough there, and he had continued doing so
after she died, although by this time its inhab-
itant was a former missionary in the South
American Missionary Society, named Dorothea
Wedgwood, commonly known as Thea. She had
worked for a number of years in Paraguay,
and more recently had devoted herself to looking after the two elderly ladies in the Round
House, one of whom was her aunt, until they
died.

On his visits, Rupert had noted the somewhat

overgrown appearance of the large garden and orchard, and had already started work on it, reclaiming the derelict patches and cutting down the hedges. He stayed for three or four weeks on this occasion, and looked with some satisfaction at the result of his labours before travelling north for the prostatectomy a surgeon friend was to perform on him. In every way it had been a satisfying visit.

He was seventy years old by this time, but there was no-one to take his place in Saiburi, so he went back.

That he was overdue for retirement, and what he would do then had already been exercising the minds of Humphrey and Helen. They discussed the matter together, agreed how an annexe to their own home could be built, and told him about it. They wanted to make a 'Grandpa flat' for him, they said. But he explained that, while deeply appreciating their intention, it would not be necessary. On his retirement he was going to marry Dorothea Wedgwood, and go to live with her in the Round House.

* * *

But he could not retire yet. The situation in Saiburi was becoming critical, with the Government ruling that any forty-bedded hospital must have three qualified doctors increasingly difficult to fulfil. Two or three missionary doctors had left, or were leaving, for family or other reasons, and he was needed. Then a temporary arrangement was decided on that would free him to go home.

A doctor from Manorom would be appointed to fill the gap until reinforcements arrived from the homeland – and there was good reason to believe that they would arrive before too long. Meanwhile, Rupert could make his arrangements for returning to England, which he did not hesitate to do. He not only made arrangements for returning to England, but for his marriage to Dorothea as well. The date was fixed: the wedding was to take place on 20 September at Emmanuel Church, Wimbledon, and the banns were being read.

Then the unexpected, and the unwelcome, happened.

The reinforcements from the homelands could not come because the Thai Government would no longer issue work permits to foreign doctors. There were now sufficient qualified Thai to meet all the medical needs in the country said the government.

'But we know of no Thai Christian doctors who would come to out-of-the-way Saiburi. It has accordingly been decided to close the hospital in mid-November . . . and I have been asked to stay on till then.' The wards were packed. How could he leave in such circumstances? But what about Dorothea?

Reluctantly he put through a telephone call to the Round House in the Isle of Wight and explained the situation.

Not for nothing had the bride-to-be herself been a missionary – and she had had her own personal commission regarding their marriage: 'Your ministry is to provide a happy retirement

for My servant.' It would not be a *happy*
retirement for him if he left the work at this
stage. Whatever embarrassments there might
be for her in cancelling the wedding arrangements at the last minute, Rupert had put his
hand to the plough and he must finish the
furrow.

'I understand,' was the reassuring message
he got over the phone, and he turned back to
the task on hand – treating the patients who
were already in the hospital, and closing down
the wards, one by one.

It was a traumatic time, not only for the missionaries, but perhaps even more for the national
staff who had worked in the hospital for years,
and must now be made redundant.

'Our own trained nursing assistants are
mostly very good, but their certificates are
not recognised by the Government, and there
are not many suitable places available for them
in private hospitals.' And there was another
even deeper concern which Rupert voiced in
the letter he wrote to his large circle of friends
and supporters.

'Now what happens to the 600-odd leprosy
patients who are treated in our clinics? And who
will care for the severely ill when our ten-bed
leprosy wing has to close? We do not know the
answer, and I am sure that the public health
officials of Pattani County have no answer, as
non-Christian clinics and hospitals do not want
anything to do with them. Almost all those who
have turned to Christ from Islam have been
through the leprosy ministry, and now to leave

them uncared for is appalling.' Yet there seemed
no answer to the problem.*

'The whole of South Thailand is buzzing with the
news of our impending closure ... and it remains
to be seen whether we fizzle out, or go out with
a bang! But we do want to spend the last three
months buying up the opportunity of gospelising
the south, and of getting yet more Gospel literature, tapes, and New Testaments into circulation.'

And in the event, they went out with a bang, not
a fizzle. A final closure celebration was arranged
in the auditorium of the Municipal Council on
the first of November (a 'Farewell Feast', Rupert
called it), to which all ex-patients, ex-staff, local
dignataries, staff of Government hospitals in the
area, and others were invited. Not surprisingly,
the central figure was 'Uncle Ru', tall, upright
as ever, smiling rather whimsically as he bowed
his head to receive the garland of flowers that
must be draped around his neck – 'Uncle Ru'
who could always be relied on, the unflappable,
the one who somehow had exemplified in his
life the confidence in the faithfulness of God to
which he so often referred. And he hadn't taken
his hand off the plough until he got to the very
end of the furrow.

* * *

* A week after the closing of the hospital in Saiburi part
of it was re-opened, as a ten-bed hospital for leprosy
patients. Only one doctor was required for such a small
unit and Dr Graham Roberts remained on, enabling the
leprosy work to continue.

Rupert arrived at Gatwick Airport on the eighth of November, and was met by Humphrey. Ten days later he walked down the aisle of Emmanuel Church, Wimbledon, from which he had been sent out as a missionary nearly fifty years before, his animated bride on his arm, to enter the last stage of his earthly pilgrimage. It was a very contented period, with the never-ending job of subduing the large garden of the Round House, singing in the choir of the church in Newport, praying steadily with Dorothea at the appointed times for the people on his list, and the places where he had worked, and now for the churches on the island. A stream of correspondence flowed in and out of the Round House, and there were red letter days when suddenly and unexpectedly communications arrived from a ward orderly on the Tibetan border who was now a doctor, and from the pastor in Java, telling how Rupert's works were following him.

Rupert enjoyed it all, and the years were studded with anniversaries, which he never allowed to be overlooked – birthdays, the opening of the Holy Light Clinic in Hwalung, Humphrey's graduation, their own wedding day. As the days approached he would say, 'We must celebrate,' and if Dorothea asked how, she always knew what the answer would be, and her mind flew to what she should put in the sandwiches.

'What shall we do?'

The answer was always the same.

'Let's go for a good long walk,' said Rupert.

PILGRIM IN CHINA

Phyllis Thompson

Phyllis Thompson is a remarkable woman: her books, numbering about thirty, have been widely-read and translated. Her recent eightieth birthday found her still writing; yet in spite of much urging, this gracious lady had shown a consistent reluctance to record the thrilling story of her own years in China. *"I've something more important to write about than myself!"* she would declare.

Now, at last, she has written *A Pilgrim in China* written in the form of letters to her publisher — Edward England and recording her own story of a call from God that demanded a response. Despite her remonstrations that she had "achieved very little" her life story is full of events, experiences and challenges which make inspiring reading.

Phyllis Thompson has written around 30 books, many of which have been translated into other languages, on people as diverse as Gladys Aylward and Madame Guyon, and of Christian societies from the London City Mission to the Gideons.

Highland Books

0 946616 39 6

ISOBEL KUHN

A New Biography by
Lois Hoadley Dick

The inspiring story of the bestselling missionary author who answered God's call to the Lisu people of China.

Isobel was making her mark in the theatre, social and academic world when, through her mother's prayers and after a tragic romance, she discovered peace with God.

After reading about Hudson Taylor and the China Inland Mission, she felt a call to China. There she married John Kuhn whom she had first met during her training at Moody.

Together they faced hardships, long separations, severe illness and war. Her experiences provided the basis of her popular books, including *By Searching*. She died in 1957 with her husband by her side.

Highland Books

0 946616 39 6

A STUDY IN SPIRITUAL POWER

An Appreciation of E. J. H. Nash (Bash)

Edited by John Eddison

E. J. H. Nash died in April 1982, aged nearly 84, after a life-long service of bringing the gospel to English public schools. A number of contributors to this book give a picture of 'Bash' as he was affectionately called, warts and all, and ask why his ministry and life were so important, and what we can learn from them today.

"That single-minded dedication to his Lord, which I saw so clearly in Bash, has been the greatest single influence on my own life."

Michael Green

"A giant in spiritual status, a strong man in leadership, and a man of steel in the face of evil."

Dick Lucas

Highland Books

0 946616 84 1

FIRE IN THE HILL

H. H. Osborn

The revival which spread from Rwanda

Many people have heard of the revival in East Africa – some know of its close association with the Ruanda Mission – but few know of its beginnings.

The fire of revival had been smouldering for some years before it burst out in the hills of Rwanda and South West Uganda in the mid 1930s. From there it spread to East Africa and beyond and for 20 years it transformed the life of the growing churches as well as the lives of the missionaries.

This is the story of how, through triumph and pain, God revealed something of his ways of working which remain, in a special way, the heritage of the Ruanda Mission.

Dr Osborn is a former missionary and for eight years was chairman of the Ruanda Mission Council.

Highland Books

0 946616 79 5

EVERY LIFE A PLAN
OF GOD

J. Oswald Sanders

No circumstance comes to pass by chance, although its significance may not be apparent at te time.

* Does God have an ideal and detailed will and plan for every life?
* Is this a valid concept or is it only a view that has been read into Scriptures which does not in fact teach it?
* If there is such a plan, surely it is of paramount importance that we get to know it.

THIS BOOK WILL TELL YOU HOW

J. Oswald Sanders, a missionary statesman with an international ministry of Bible teaching, demonstrates how the circumstances surrounding our lives are not accidental, but devised by an all-wise and loving Father.

Highland Books

0 946616 83 3

WONG MING DAO

Day by Day

A Chinese Christian's call to
a devout and holy life

Highland Books have commissioned this translation of daily readings by Wong Ming-Dao to give English readers a glimpse of the faith which sustained him through twenty-three years of imprisonment and his wife through twenty years.

The ability of Chinese Christians to maintain their witness, as they have done through decades of pressure, is undoubtedly due – at least in part – to the faithfulness, tenacity and courage of such outstanding leaders as Wong Ming-Dao. His unwillingness to compromise is one of the secrets of his strong leadership and can be seen in these writings.

Highland Books

0 946616 43 4

DAWN 2000

Discipling A Whole Nation

Jim Montgomery

A book destined to make a significant measurable impact on the evangelisation of the world.

What kind of person could possibly write a book on 7 million churches which have not yet been planted?

What kind of person could even think of such a thing?

Jim Montgomery is that person. This book, the first definitive treatment of the DAWN movement, will certainly take its place as one of the premier missiological works of the closing years of the 20th Century. It is a book which has all the marks of a classic even before it gets to the bookshop.

The author is founder and president of Dawn Ministries. He and his wife Lyn served with Overseas Crusades for 27 years in Asia. It was during his 13 years in the Philippines that he developed the DAWN strategy.

Highland Books

9 046616 73 6